BRANCH LINE BYWAYS

VOLUME THREE

South Wales

Ian L. Wright

FRONT COVER: On 31 May 1958 0-4-2T 1471 prepares to depart for Penygraig from the bay on the up side of Llantrisant station. *Photo: Ian L. Wright*

BACK COVER, TOP: 0-6-0PT 3786 nears Machen with the 7.07 pm from Newport to Brecon in July 1962. *Photo: Alan Jarvis*

BACK COVER, BOTTOM: Once again in 1962 with the 7.07 pm Newport to Brecon, this time with 0-6-0 2218 in charge as it arrives at Bassaleg. *Photo: Alan Jarvis*

TITLE PAGE: Old Ynysybwl Halt on 13 March 1948. GWR 0-4-2T 1461 and driving trailer 114 wait at the bridge with an afternoon Ynysybwl Branch train. *Photo: Ian L. Wright*

First published 1988

Designed by Nigel Trevena
Typeset by Delta Graphics, Falmouth, Cornwall
Halftone photo reproduction by Oxford Litho Plates Ltd, Botley, Oxford
Printed by Century Litho, Penryn, Cornwall
Bound by Booth Bookbinders, Penryn, Cornwall

©Text, Ian L. Wright
©Photographs, accredited photographers

No part of this publication may be reproduced in any form or by any means without the prior written permission of the publishers

ISBN 0 906899 30 3

Published by
ATLANTIC TRANSPORT
PUBLISHERS
Waterside House Falmouth Road
Penryn Cornwall TR10 8BE
England

The Author

Ian L. Wright NDD ATD was born in Barry, Glamorgan, and grew up in South Wales sharing his father's love of railways which continues to this day. He is a photographer with a keen interest in architecture, and the author of articles in the railway and canal press. His LNER book in Atlantic's BRANCH LINE MEMORIES series was published in 1986. Ian has spent many years of his life teaching in Northamptonshire where he was Head of the Art Department at one of the county's comprehensive schools until retirement in 1986.

Note

The mileages quoted are those given in the service timetables of the Great Western Railway. Track layout diagrams published by R. A. Cooke have also been consulted. On South Wales Valley lines up and down trains refer to the direction of travel up or down the valleys. Maps are not to scale. Spelling of place names in this book follows the style used in the GWR timetables in 1947. The name "Llantrissant & Taff Vale Junction" is the legal form of the name of the railway company concerned.

Bibliography

The following sources were consulted during the preparation of this volume and are recommended for further reading:

D. S. M. BARRIE: *Taff Vale Railway;*
  Oakwood Press
  Brecon & Merthyr Railway;
  Oakwood Press
  Regional History Vol.12 South Wales;
  David & Charles
ERIC R. MOUNTFORD: *Cardiff Railway;*
  Oakwood Press
COLIN CHAPMAN: *Cowbridge Railway;*
  Oxford Publishing Co.
  Llantrissant & Taff Vale Junction Railway; Unpublished Paper
BRIAN J. MILLER: *South Wales Railways at the Grouping;* D. Brown, Cowbridge
JAMES PAGE: *Forgotten Railways South Wales;* David & Charles
SERVICE and PUBLIC TIMETABLES of the GWR and BR (Western Region)
Railway Magazine
Railway World
Trains Illustrated
Stephenson Locomotive Society, 'Last Train Souvenir Brochures' and Rail Tour Notes
R. A. COOKE: *Track Layout Diagrams of the GWR and BR WR*

Maps: Some lines have been omitted and certain junctions have been left unidentified in the interests of clarity.

Acknowledgements

I would like to express my thanks to the photographers and owners of collections who have contributed pictures to this book and especially Ben Ashworth, Derek Chaplin, Alan Jarvis, Rev R. W. A. Jones and Dick Riley.

Dick Riley, Colin Chapman, Roland Pittard and the late Eric Mountford have helped generously with information and advice, and I am grateful to Russell Twisk, editor of The Listener *for permission to reproduce part of the 1962 BBC broadcast talk "The Poacher's Express" by Huw Ballard Thomas.*

A final word of thanks to Nigel Trevena for suggesting the idea of this book and for his encouragement along the way.

Foreword

Now that it has become commonplace for a whole book to be published on one minor branch line, the reader may sympathise with me in putting together this collection. In the tight confines of a modest book, which lines do you choose and group coherently? How much history, how much comment, how many pictures, how much space for reminiscence and how much detail? I have had to edit myself severely in one of the most involved railway regions in the world. That is why a favourite junction may have to be left out or a neighbouring branch line edited away. To the authors and publishers listed below I acknowledge my indebtedness in the preparation of the text and captions. My thanks are also extended to Mr John Davies and his staff, Provincial Manager (Wales), British Rail, Cardiff.

Dedication

To Pat — who survived a year of stepping over timetables, books and photographs with good humour.

ABOVE: A lively evocation of steam on the Brecon & Merthyr line at Brecon in May 1953. GWR Collett 0-6-0 2249 is on the 1.10 pm SO Brecon to Hereford and Ivatt Class 2 2-6-0 46518 is in the bay with the 1.20 pm to Moat Lane. Behind the Hereford train is the B&M station building of 1871 which once housed the company's general offices.
Photo: Derek Chaplin

RIGHT: The GWR station nameboard on the Joint Line at Cefn Coed, with a good feeling for vice versa, recalls the old ownerships in August 1956. *Photo: Ian L. Wright*

Brecon-Pontsticill Jcn

ORIGIN: **Brecon & Merthyr Tydfil Junction Railway, incorporating Rumney Railway, and exercising running powers over Rhymney Railway and GWR**

LENGTH: **47m 6ch Brecon-Newport High Street**

OPENED:
23 April 1863 (Passenger & Freight: Brecon-Pant)
1 September 1868 (Passenger: Brecon-Newport Dock Street)

CLOSED:
31 December 1962 (Passenger: Brecon-Newport High Street)
31 December 1962 (Freight: Pengam-Bedwas)
5 August 1963 (Freight: Pant-Deri Junction)
4 May 1964 (Freight: Brecon-Pant)
23 August 1965 (Freight: Deri Junction-Bargoed North Junction)

RULING GRADIENT: **1 in 38**

BELOW: Rural Talyllyn Junction on 18 August 1956 where passengers from the 11.10 am Newport-Brecon train, brought in by Ivatt Class 2 2-6-0 46521, are crossing the barrow walk for the Mid Wales connection — the 1.25 pm Brecon-Moat Lane Junction with sister engine 46510 in charge.
Photo: Ian L. Wright

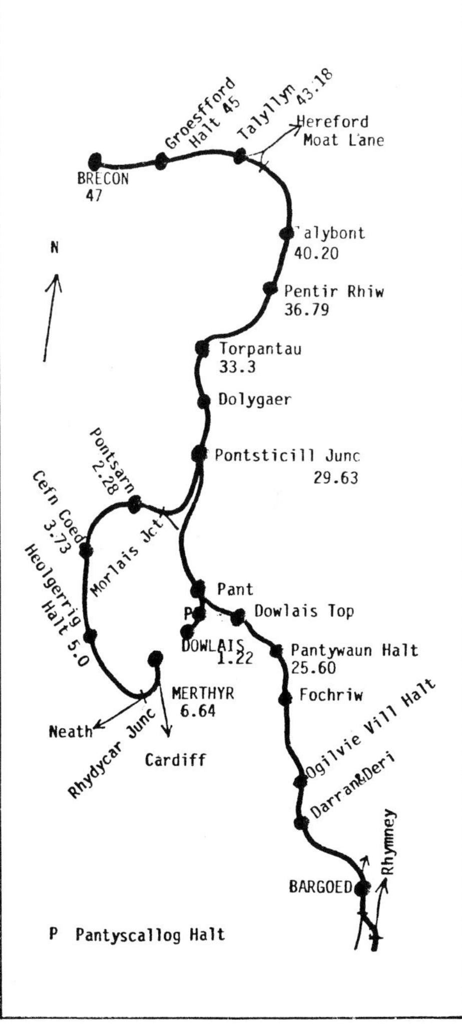

An evocative photograph was my first encounter with the Brecon & Merthyr line. I was still at school when a picture of a Dean Goods 0-6-0 appeared in an article in my father's Railway Magazine. The Dean was struggling to the top of the Seven Mile Bank with a Brecon-Newport passenger train, her single line progress at nearly 1,300 feet being framed by a backdrop of wild mountains. The almost forgotten photographer who stood on that lonely saddle above Torpantau Tunnel was Oscar Elsden, a man who knew a dramatic viewpoint when he saw one.

The 47 mile journey from Brecon to Newport was, by anyones standards, one of the most romantic in Britain. At up to 2 hours 40 minutes it was also one of the slowest. There were, of course, 22 stations, 19 miles of single line, a number of junctions with connections to make, and two summits of over 1,300 feet to surmount in conditions that could be cruel in winter. The B&M stations averaged just two miles apart and made a contribution to what has been called 'Stopping Train Britain'. This endeared the legendary B&M line to its communities until they forsook the railway for the bus.

Though the line presented less of a byway image as it busied itself with coal from the Rhymney Valley to Newport Docks, I have given the whole B&M a little space. At Pontsticill, Pant and Aberbargoed Junction I have broken the Newport journey to look

at the branches to Merthyr, Dowlais and New Tredegar. The Caerphilly Branch is more conveniently described in the 'Pontypridd Branches'.

ABOVE: The Mid Wales line connection, Talyllyn Junction on 26 March 1951. This picture of GWR 0-6-0 887 (ex Cambrian Railways 89) was taken by making a quick dash off the 11.00 am Newport-Brecon train which Dean Goods 2538 had just brought in to Talyllyn. 887 was at the head of the 1.20 pm Brecon-Moat Lane train which called at 25 idyllic stations including Three Cocks Junction, Builth Wells and Llanidloes. *Photo: Ian L. Wright*

Brecon-Pontsticill Jcn

At Talybont-on-Usk the B&M line crossed the floor of the Vale of Usk in a setting of superb pastoral and mountain scenery. There was once a good traffic in cattle here and the station dealt with a few village passengers and those who came for the fishing. The Usk Hotel, seen behind the signal and cattle dock, was nicely placed for those with time to spare until train time. In the grass grown yard at Talybont a one-road stone built engine shed survived; a reminder of banking days on the B&M. The station building still exists as an outdoor activities centre.

Standing in Talybont station loop at a mere 385 feet above sea level and with tanks just replenished from the stone faced water column, GWR 0-6-0 panniers 9676 and 4690 prepare to lift a Merthyr bound freight train over 900 feet in seven miles on the unrelenting climb at 1 in 38 to Torpantau Summit on 29 August 1963. *Photo: B. J. Ashworth*

Halfway up the Seven Mile Bank was Pentir Rhiw with its signalbox and loop and miniscule island platform. It was a beautiful setting, the reservoir occupying the flooded Glyn Collwng to the west of the line and the afforested slopes of Tor y Foel rising to the east, but wilder places were yet to come. Put in the B&MR timetable as a conditional stop in 1909,

Pentir Rhiw was a passing place where the signalman looked after the loop and a funicular-like runaway siding that ran crazily up the mountainside. He also issued tickets from a window in the signalbox.

Full regulator at Pentir Rhiw on 4 September 1963 as 9676 raises the echoes in Glyn Collwng on her way up the Seven Mile Bank with a freight train

for Merthyr. Passenger trains were allowed 28-30 minutes for the 7¼ mile climb to Torpantau and freight trains 44 minutes. Down the bank the allowance was 15 minutes for passenger trains and 35 minutes for freight, exclusive of time spent by freight crews in obeying the instructions of stop boards.
Photo: B. J. Ashworth

Brecon-Pontsticill Jcn

Torpantau, the Welsh Slochd, was one of Britain's loneliest railway locations. Walk away to the flanks of the Beacons for just five minutes and you saw the train as a tiny thing in the landscape. At 1,313 feet above sea level it made an interesting comparison with Slochd Summit (1,315 feet) on the Highland main line, and the 666 yard Torpantau Tunnel had the distinction of being Britain's highest railway tunnel. It is best remembered for its breathtaking eastern exit. Suddenly out of its inky blackness came a marvellous panorama of Glyn Collwng far below.

Torpantau could see a brief flurry of activity at 1.05 pm as two passenger trains crossed there — the 11.00 am from Newport and the 12.15 pm from Brecon; a momentary brush with civilisation among the Beacons and then silence returned to the mountains.

<table>
<tr><td>7350</td><td>BRITISH RLYS (W)   BRITISH RLYS (W)
Talybont on Usk Talybont on Usk
TO
TALYLLYN
THIRD CLASS
8d Z Fare 8d Z
Talyllyn   Talyllyn
FOR CONDITIONS FOR CONDITIONS
SEE BACK   SEE BACK C.L</td><td>7350</td></tr>
</table>

ABOVE: In deepest wartime, on 12 August 1943, GWR Dean 0-6-0 2569 was recorded near the head of Glyn Collwng with the 2.00 pm Brecon to Newport train about to enter Torpantau Tunnel at the top of the Seven Mile Bank from Talybont-on-Usk.
Photo: V. R. Webster

RIGHT: On 2 November 1962, a few weeks before the end of the passenger service, the signalman stands in the loop to exchange the staff with a freight train for Merthyr headed by GWR 0-6-0PT 9676. Note the slate-hung gable end of Torpantau signalbox, a necessary protection in a hostile environment.
Photo: B. J. Ashworth

M.	C.	M.	C.	STATIONS.	Station No.	Gradient 1 in
…	…	…	…	Newport(W.Mendalgief)		
…	…	…	…	Park Sidings ..		
…	…	…	.	Bassaleg Loop ….		
…	…	—	—	**Newport (High St.)**	2680	
0	0	2	62	Bassaleg Junction		
0	23	3	5	**Bassaleg**		110 R
1	38	4	20	**Rhiwderin** …. ….		82 R
3	41	6	23	**Church Road** ..		290 R
4	47	7	29	Machen Loco. Shops		,,
5	1	7	63	**Machen** …. ..		,,
6	70	9	52	**Trethomas** .. ….		260 R
7	69	10	51	**Bedwas**		,,
9	38	12	20	Barry Junction ….	7706	234 R
12	14	15	26	**Maesycwmmer** ..	7596	270 R
13	22	16	4	Fleur-de-lis South ….	7711	184 R
13	44	16	26	Fleur-de-lis Sidings ..	7714	184 R
13	61	16	43	**Fleur-de-lis pl'tform**		
14	30	17	12	**Pengam (Mon.)** ….	7582	96 R
14	60	17	42	Britannia Colly. Sdg. N.		96 R
				Gilfach Quarry ….		96 R
15	10	17	72	Aber Bargoed Junction	7720	96 R
15	34	18	16	Gwaelodywaen Colly.		96 R
16	0	18	62	Bargoed Colliery Halt		96 R
16	26	19	8	**Aber Bargoed** ….	7551	99 R
17	21	20	3	**Cwmsyfiog** .	7574	99 R
17	55	20	37	Elliot Pit …. ….	7723	99 R
18	39	21	21	**New Tredegar** ..	7600	98 R
19	23	22	5	New Tredegar Coll. P.		
19	55	22	37	New Tredegar Colliery	7725	98 R
19	66	22	48	McLaren No. 1 Colly.	7727	98 R
19	73	22	55	McLaren Colly. Plat.		
19	79	22	61	**Abertysswg** ….	7556	98 R
20	70	23	52	**Rhymney (Lower)**	7616	98 R
…	…	18	54	Bargoed South Jc. ←‹‹‹	8125	96 R
…	…	18	68	**Bargoed**	7557	94 R
…	…	18	74	Bargoed North Junction	8127	94 R
…	…	20	45	Groesfaen South ..	8130	64 R
…	…	20	12	Groesfaen Colliers' P'tfm		64 R
…	…	20	62	Darran Pit		47 R
…	…	20	73	**Darran & Deri** ….	7575	47 R
		21	20	Ogilvie Colliery ..		43 R
		21	15	Deri Junction ….	8133	43 R
		21	67	Ogilvie Colliery Halt		43 R
		23	68	**Fochriw** .. ….	7583	300 R
		25	20	Pantywaen Junction	8138	75 F
			—	Stop Board …. ….		
		26	46	Dowlais Top Junction	8140	50 F
		26	57	Dowlais Top Clay Sidings	8141	56 F
		26	49	**Dowlais Top** .	7578	300 F
—	—	…	…	**Dowlais (Central)**	7577	L
0	71	…	…	**Pantyscallog** ….	7664	80 R
1	22	28	22	**Pant** …. …. ….	7601	231 F
		29	26	Tylerybont Kilns ..		100 R
		29	63	**Pontsticill Jct.** ←‹‹‹	7608	198 F
		31	36	**Dolygaer** .. .		47 R
		33	3	**Torpantau** ….		47 R
		—	—	Stop Board		38 F
		—	—	Stop Board …. ….		
		36	79	**Pentir Rhiw** ..		38 F
		10	20	**Talybont-on-Usk**		49 R
		—	—	Talyllyn Junction East		
		43	18	**Talyllyn Junction**		73 F
..	…	47	6	Brecon		

V 3 minutes from Bassaleg Junction. **W**

The *Distance from* column at lower left is headed **Distance from Dowlais (Central).**

BELOW: The 6.15 pm Brecon to Newport train is brought in to Pontsticill Junction on 22 August 1957 by pannier tank 3634 of Ebbw Junction shed. Built in 1939 the engine was a familiar performer on the B&M lines all its working life until it was put into store in 1963. A few minutes before arriving here this train had crossed a Hereford bound freight at Torpantau hauled by two 3600 Class pannier tanks with empty ammonia tank wagons from Dowlais to Widnes in the train. The 6.15 pm from Brecon was a popular service, being the last departure of the day for Newport. Rail still exists here in the form of Rheilffordd Mynydd Brycheiniog, the narrow gauge Brecon Mountain Railway which was opened in 1980 along the B&M trackbed from Pant. *Photo: Ian L. Wright*

THE POACHER'S EXPRESS
SOME THOUGHTS ON THE NEWPORT TO BRECON 1962

… "But the most exciting thing about the Newport to Brecon in those days was not the short run we made on it from Fochriw to Bargoed, but the thought of the worlds to which it linked us. South, there were the hissing collieries, the arrogant villages pretending they were towns, the bargain emporiums, and Newport, bustling and booming — the gateway to London, to England, the world! And north, there was Brecon, cool and cathedraled, with boats on the river and muffins for tea in an oak-quiet café. And to get there the little train whistled and groaned its way — sometimes two engines at a time for the steepest of gradients — all that singing way through the sweep of the Beacons, past the silver-fished reservoirs, the clusters of pine trees, and the breathtaking beauty of mountain and river.

Where else in the world could you pass through so many moods in one train journey of less than three hours? The names of the places alone must have been dreamed up by some remote god of poetry: Machen and Maesycymmer, Pant and Pontsticill, Talybont and Talyllyn, Morgannwg and Mynwy, Brycheiniog and all.

The 'Poacher's Express': that was the favourite name of the Newport to Brecon. For all through the valley you would pick up dust-filled men laden with rods for fishing and traps for rabbits, bound for the fresh air and spoils of the fair county of Brecon. They were brave men. It's one thing to boast of your exploits, and your skill on the journey up in the morning — and another to have to prove it to the same audience on the way home in the evening.

Soon the old Newport to Brecon will be no more. Some will mourn its passing as a matter of principle; a few because it will deprive them of many an hour of pleasure; others, like myself, because it will be like removing the backbone from one of those trout you caught in the rivers of Talybont. For that line gave a shape and meaning and a flow of life to our childhood. True, it took us away to far-distant, alien places, yet it was always there to bring us back again. Now we shall swoop through the valleys in snarling new cars, and climb the steepest gradients of the Beacons with scarcely a cough from the gears: and in that fact alone we shall realise how much times have changed. But it would be a hard man who wouldn't permit us a moment of sadness that it had to be so."

Extract from BBC broadcast talk, 'The Poacher's Express', by Huw Ballard Thomas, *The Listener* 14 June 1962 and reproduced by kind permission of the Editor.

Merthyr Branch

<table>
<tr><td>ORIGIN:</td><td>Brecon & Merthyr Railway</td></tr>
<tr><td>LENGTH:</td><td>6m 20ch (Pontsticill-Rhydycar Junction)</td></tr>
<tr><td>OPENED:</td><td>1 August 1868 (Passenger & Freight: Pontsticill-Merthyr (Rhydycar Junction))</td></tr>
<tr><td>CLOSED:</td><td>13 November 1961 (Passenger)
4 May 1964 (Freight: Pontsticill-Vaynor Quarry)
3 October 1966 (Freight: Vaynor Quarry-Rhydycar Junction)</td></tr>
<tr><td>RULING GRADIENT:</td><td>1 in 45</td></tr>
</table>

The Brecon & Merthyr Tydfil Junction Railway had been seen as part of a grand design linking Wales from north to south and in 1859 three local lines were incorporated; the Hereford Hay & Brecon, the Mid Wales, and the B&M. The Brecon & Merthyr's immediate aim was to link Brecon with the coal and iron producing region of Dowlais and Merthyr.

The B&M reached Brecon by acquiring the western end of the Hay Railway and reconstructing the Talyllyn to Brecon portion as a standard gauge line. The B&M had been completed from Brecon to Pant in 1863 but financial disasters ruined the contractors Savin & Ward and left the Merthyr Branch incomplete. It was eventually built and opened to Cefn Coed in 1867 but the opening to Rhydycar Junction on the Vale of Neath line was delayed until Cefn Coed viaduct could be completed in 1868.

From Pontsticill Junction the single line Merthyr Branch ran parallel with the Newport line but descended steeply at 1 in 50 into the limestone gorge carved by the Taff Fechan river. At Morlais Junction the single line was met by the double track of the Merthyr, Tredegar & Abergavenny line of the London & North Western Railway (later London Midland & Scottish Railway) which had just emerged from Morlais Tunnel. To gain access to Merthyr from Dowlais (not much more than a mile away but around 500 feet higher) the LNWR got the agreement of the B&MR for the junction at Morlais. From Morlais Junction to Rhydycar Junction the line became B&M and LNW joint property and the LNW paid retrospectively half the B&M's bill for building the line, a particularly difficult and expensive piece of engineering with viaducts at Pontsarn and Cefn Coed, both of which still exist. The LNWR began its services between Abergavenny and Merthyr on 1 June 1879. The route of the Merthyr Branch made a bizarre shape on the railway map as it followed the twists of the Taff Fechan gorge, encircling Merthyr through almost every point of the compass, and finally entering Merthyr High Street station from the south, originally by running powers over the 44 chains of the GWR.

ABOVE: Pontsticill Junction was at the lower end of the Taff Fechan reservoir where the train still ran above the 1,000 ft contour and there is a superb prospect of the distant Beacons. Here the Old Red Sandstone gives way to the Carboniferous limestone of the coalfield edge and the rock faces here and at Vaynor have been extensively quarried for fluxing stone for the iron industry and for roadstone and rail ballast. This passenger's eye view shows Pontsticill on 30 August 1962 as GWR 0-6-0PT 3747 enters with a Brecon-Newport train. The Merthyr Branch platform is on the extreme right but by this time the passenger service to Merthyr had been withdrawn.
Photo: B. J. Ashworth

Turning to the LMS sector of the Joint Line partnership through the limestone gorge, what could be more exciting to the devotees of Crewe than to see a Webb 0-6-2 Coal Tank battling up the 1 in 45 through Pontsarn with an Abergavenny passenger train, or an ex-LNW 0-8-0 hauling an even longer rake of LMS stock over Cefn Coed viaduct on Abergavenny Market day. But this oddly isolated part of the LNW system which enabled the Euston forces to get a foothold in the South Wales valleys was in the end to be nationalised, Westernised and rationalised. After passing to the Western Region in late 1948 the MT&A line retained its LMS character for a while, but from 22 November 1954 all through goods traffic on the MT&A was diverted to ex GWR routes leaving the passenger service only. Abergavenny loco shed was closed and the remaining passenger services were worked from the ex GWR shed at Merthyr, all return workings except one being handled by auto fitted panniers. Familiar engines on the Abergavenny auto turns between 1955 and the end of the passenger service in 1958 were 6408, 6411, 6423, 6433 and 6436.

ABOVE: The old order changeth. Crewe bows to Swindon at Cefn Coed as a Merthyr 6400 Class 0-6-0PT bound for Abergavenny Junction propels its GWR type auto train into Cefn Coed on this former LMS service. The scene was recorded in October 1956. *Photo: Derek Chaplin*

Merthyr Branch

Cefn Coed, the principal station on the Merthyr Branch, was a staff station and crossing place with full freight handling facilities, the goods shed being next to the stone-built station house. Pontsarn for Vaynor, the other station on the Joint Line, was a single platform affair with wooden buildings and not a crossing place. In the days of simpler pleasures it could be thronged by Sunday school children on chapel outings. Pontsarn did not survive as a station and in modern times it became an unstaffed halt. Another halt, Heolgerrig, served a community on the western edge of Merthyr. An important freight on the Merthyr branch was the traffic in stone from Vaynor Quarry siding.

A compelling end to a run over the Merthyr Branch in 1951 would be your arrival at Brunel's timber-built terminal station at Merthyr High Street which was opened by the Vale of Neath Railway in 1853. In some ways the all-over roof was more interesting to look at during its demolition in August 1952 when rows of timber trusses stood open to the sky and light flooded into the boardwalk platforms and illuminated the pillars of the nave arcades.

Train watching at Merthyr had its peaks of entertainment. Take 30 August 1951 for example:

11.44 am A GWR 5600 Class 0-6-2T arrives in No.2 with the 10.26 am from Cardiff.

11.47 am Ivatt LMS-built 2-6-2T 41201 arrives in No.1 off the Merthyr Branch with the two open gangway Lancashire & Yorkshire Railway coaches of the 10.10 am from Abergavenny Junction.

11.48 am Station pilot GWR 292 — an ex TVR 0-6-2T — removes a van off the back of the Cardiff arrival.

11.53 am GWR 0-4-2T 1425 moves out of No.4 with the Hirwaun auto.

12.10 pm GWR 0-6-0PT 7772 leaves No.3 for the Merthyr Branch with two old GWR steam car trailers for Pontsticill and there was the certainty that when you got there it would be a Dean Goods on the front of the 11.00 am from Newport to take you over the Beacons to Brecon.

Table 123 — PONTSTICILL JUNCTION and MERTHYR — (Third class only)

Week Days only

Miles		a.m	a.m	a.m	a.m	a.m		p.m	p.m	p.m	p.m (D)	p.m	p.m (S)	p.m	p.m (S)	p.m	
	Pontsticill Junction dep	..	8 43	..	10 2	..	..	1 19	3 10	..	..	..	6 20	7 25	8 45	..	..
2¼	Pontsarn, for Vaynor	6 4	8 50	9 8	10 9	11 28	..	1 26	3 17	3 51	..	6 18	6 27	7 33	8 52	9 47	..
4	Cefn Coed	6 10	8 55	9 15	1014	1135	..	1 31	3 23	3 57	4 36	6 24	6 32	7 39	8 58	9 54	..
5	Heolgerrig Halt	..	8 59	9 20	1018	1140	..	1 35	3 27	4 2	..	6 29	6 36	7 44	9 3	9 59	..
6¼	Merthyr arr	..	9 4	9 23	1024	1147	..	1 40	3 32	4 9	4 45	6 36	6 41	7 50	9 9	10 6	..

Week Days only

Miles		a.m	a.m	a.m (D)	a.m	a.m	a.m		p.m	p.m	p.m	p.m	p.m	p.m (S)	p.m (S)	p.m	
	Merthyr dep	..	7 30	8 5	8 45	9 28	10 3	..	1210	1220	2 38	4 10	4 43	6 50	8 0	8 30	..
1¼	Heolgerrig Halt	..	7 35	8 10	..	9 33	10 8	..	1215	1225	2 43	4 16	4 48	6 55	8 5	8 35	..
2¼	Cefn Coed	6 20	7 41	8 14	8 54	9 37	1014	..	1219	1230	2 47	4 20	4 52	6 59	8 9	8 40	..
4	Pontsarn, for Vaynor	6 25	7 46	8 19	..	9 42	1019	..	1224	1235	2 52	4 28	4 58	7 4	8 14	8 45	..
6¼	Pontsticill Junction arr	..	..	8 28	..	9 49	..	..	1231	..	2 59	4 33	..	7 11	8 21	..	..

D Except Saturdays and School Holidays

S Saturdays only

WR Passenger Timetable No.123 25 September 1950

BELOW: Merthyr Branch trains at Merthyr High Street on 30 August 1951. Pannier tank 7772 is in platform 3 waiting to take out the 12.10 pm branch train to Pontsticill. Ivatt 2-6-2T 41201 with two L&Y coaches for Abergavenny Junction, will follow to Morlais Junction at 12.20 pm. By contrast, in 1987 the railway to Merthyr survives by a thread. One single line from Cardiff is all that is left, but the future is more hopeful today than at any time in the last 20 years. *Photo: Ian L. Wright*

Dowlais Branch

ORIGIN: **Brecon & Merthyr Railway**
LENGTH: **1m 22ch**
OPENED: **23 June 1869 (Passenger & Freight)**
CLOSED: **2 May 1960 (Passenger) 4 May 1964 (Freight)**
RULING
GRADIENT: **1 in 40**

BELOW: There is a tidy Great Western look to this Dowlais Branch train on 3 June 1950 as GWR 0-6-0PT 5711 stands at Dowlais Central with a smart B Set ready to move off for Pant. *Photo: Ian L. Wright*

Dowlais is not a place visitors would ordinarily visit to admire the view. At close on 1,000 feet above sea level it is bleak and much scarred by the marks of coal and iron ore exploitation and by the industrial waste of two centuries of iron making. A great deal has recently been done to clear and landscape the area for modern life and commerce. The great Dowlais Ironworks, started in 1759, brought a complication of competing railways to Dowlais, and under an Act of 1865 the B&M built a short single line branch from Pant to Dowlais to improve connections to the town and ironworks. The branch which opened in 1869, fell sharply at 1 in 40 from the rural junction at Pant. At only 1 mile 22 chains the Dowlais Branch must have been one of the shortest branch lines in Britain. It made up for this though, with some unusual train working and rolling stock.

When I visited the branch terminus in 1950 the single passenger road ended so close to the goods shed that you imagined a careless driver could have demolished the end wall! The typical single storey B&M station building, bathed in June sunshine, was still sporting some exotic B&M gas lamps of another age. A rake or two of old GWR clerestories, for the workmen's train to Bargoed, filled the siding near the one road loco shed built in 1916. Dowlais Central had begun life as 'Lloyd Street' but local people simply called it 'The Tip Station' — no offence intended — but a literal description of the site which had been formed on the waste from Dowlais Ironworks. The B&M was unable to keep the advancing LNWR out of Dowlais and a deep double-track moon landscape cutting is evidence of the LNWR's thrust from Penywern Junction to the B&M at Ivor Junction which brought LNWR trains to the branch on 1 January 1873.

There was one intermediate station on the Dowlais Branch, at Pantyscallog, opened in 1911, but later downgraded to a halt and electric staff was used between Pant and Dowlais No.1 (Ivor Junction).

There were eight passenger trips over the branch and ten on Saturdays when I travelled over the line by the 1.00 pm from Dowlais, on 30 August 1951. It was one of three workmen's trains which ran to and from Bargoed, reversing at Pant. Journey time for the trip to Pant was five minutes if terminating at the branch platform but this could extend to seven or eight minutes for the reversing manoeuvre of the workmen's trains. Our engine was GWR 217, an ex TVR 04 Class 0-6-2T coupled to a GWR bogie clerestory, a Rhymney third and a modern GWR non corridor third bringing up at the rear, and only the last vehicle was upholstered! At Pant the train ran clear of the junction which converges towards Brecon. It then backed into the 'main line' platform and 217 came off and ran round the train to take us on to Bargoed.

LEFT: In the 1930s, GWR ex Taff Vale 0-6-2T 292 is at Dowlais Central with a morning departure for the junction. This time the train is a pair of vintage GWR 4 wheelers. The striped bunting round the smoke box handrail suggests a celebration — 1935 Silver Jubilee or 1937 Coronation? *Photo: Lens of Sutton*

ABOVE: A quiet simmer for GWR 0-6-0PT 7772 outside Dowlais Central's one road shed on 3 June 1950. The original engine shed, built in 1898, came to grief in a blizzard in 1916 and this one immediately replaced it. 7772 has been working the branch line's two goods turns and the Dowlais U target is carried on the lamp bracket. At this time the Guest Keen Nettlefolds Ivor Works and ICI sidings were providing some traffic to the branch. *Photo: Rev R. W. A. Jones*

Table 122 **PANT and DOWLAIS**

Miles		Week Days only															
		a.m	a.m	a.m		p.m	p.m	p.m	p.m	p.m		p.m	p.m	p.m	p.m	
		W	S					S W	S	Ew				S	Ew		
—	Pant.....................dep	7 28	9 50	..	9 53	..	1240	1 25	2 24 3 12	3 22	..	4 40	7 27	1115 11 22	..		C High Level
¾	Pantysgallog Halt C...	7 31	9 53	..	9 58	..	1243	1 28	2 27 3 15	3 25	..	4 43	7 30	1118 11 25	..		E Except Saturdays
1½	Dowlais (Central)...arr	7 34	9 56	..	10 1	..	1246	1 32	2 30 3 18	3 28	..	4 46	7 33	1121 11 30	..		S Saturdays only

Miles		Week Days only															
		a.m	a.m	a.m		p.m	p.m	p.m	p.m		p.m	p.m	p.m		p.m	
		W	S					Ew	S				S		Ew		
—	Dowlais (Central)...dep	5 2	8 25	..	9 33	..	1220	1255	1 0 2 45	..	4 10	7 5	9 22	..	9 20	..	W Workmen's Train
¾	Pantysgallog Halt C...	5 5	8 28	..	9 36	..	1223	1258	1 5 2 48	..	4 13	7 8	9 25	..	9 23	..	
1½	Pant.....................arr	5 8	8 30	..	9 38	..	1225	1 0	1 7 2 51	..	4 15	7 10	9 27	..	9 28	..	

New Tredegar Branch

<table>
<tbody>
<tr><td>ORIGIN:</td><td>Rumney Railway, Brecon & Merthyr Tydfil Junction Railway</td></tr>
<tr><td>LENGTH:</td><td>3m 29ch (Aberbargoed Junction-New Tredegar)
(5m 60ch Rhymney Lower)</td></tr>
<tr><td>OPENED:</td><td>14 June 1865 (Passenger: Pengam-Bassaleg-Newport Dock Street)
16 April 1866 (Passenger: Pengam-Rhymney)
B&M coal trains Rhymney-Newport authorised in 1867</td></tr>
<tr><td>CLOSED:</td><td>14 April 1930 (Passenger & Freight: Rhymney Lower-New Tredegar)
31 December 1962 (Passenger: New Tredegar-Newport)
31 December 1962 (Freight: Aberbargoed Junction-New Tredegar)
31 December 1962 (Freight: Bedwas-Fleur de lis Junction)
6 November 1967 (Freight: Pengam-Fleur de lis Junction)</td></tr>
<tr><td>RULING GRADIENT:</td><td>1 in 96</td></tr>
</tbody>
</table>

The Rhymney B&M Branch (later to be called the New Tredegar Branch) took on the status of a branch line in 1868 when the B&M's Northern Section was extended down the Bargoed Rhymney valley to meet the Southern Section at Aberbargoed Junction. This engagement with the Rhymney Railway had been made possible by running powers over the RR between Deri Junction and Bargoed South Junction.

The impoverished B&M had made an astute move by its purchase in 1863 of the 'Old Rumney', a horse tramroad reincorporated as a railway in 1861. By 1867 this Rhymney-Bassaleg part of the B&M was enjoying a busy life of its own, carrying lucrative coal and iron traffic to Newport Docks for export. The environmental cost to this coalfield valley was huge — close packed terraced communities hemmed in by tips of colliery waste. Not easily forgotten are Bargoed's smoking rows of coke ovens and — ultimate outrage — the vast whale-like Aberbargoed Tip, now well afforested and conjuring thoughts of Switzerland among the more imaginative.

The B&M Rhymney Branch started at Rhymney Ironworks, descending the eastern side of the valley through New Tredegar to Aberbargoed and on to Bedwas, Machen and Bassaleg. Rhymney (Lower) GWR, the passenger terminus, stood close to fields that had not been completely engulfed by McLaren No.2 Colliery. The branch was single, Rhymney-Abertysswg, and double from McLaren No.1 pit all the way to Aberbargoed Junction and through to Bassaleg. Mining subsidences troubled the railway over the years. In 1928 a landslide overcame the line and the GWR closed the New Tredegar-Rhymney (Lower) section in 1930 and reduced New Tredegar-Aberbargoed Junction to single track. New Tredegar passenger trains ran all-stations through to Newport and were an almost wholly separate concern from the Brecon trains. The image was smartly Great Western — a pannier tank at the head of three GWR non-corridors and intermediate stations on the branch were at Cwmsyfiog and Aberbargoed.

ABOVE: Several of the trains on the New Tredegar Branch were colliers' trains to and from Bedwas Colliery. This one, leaving New Tredegar at 2.38 pm, ran down the Rhymney Valley to Machen where it was parked in the Caerphilly bay. This was my only trip on the branch, made on 23 October 1954, and the engine was GWR 0-6-0PT 3714. The station's cash box stands nonchalantly on the barrow.
Photo: Ian L. Wright

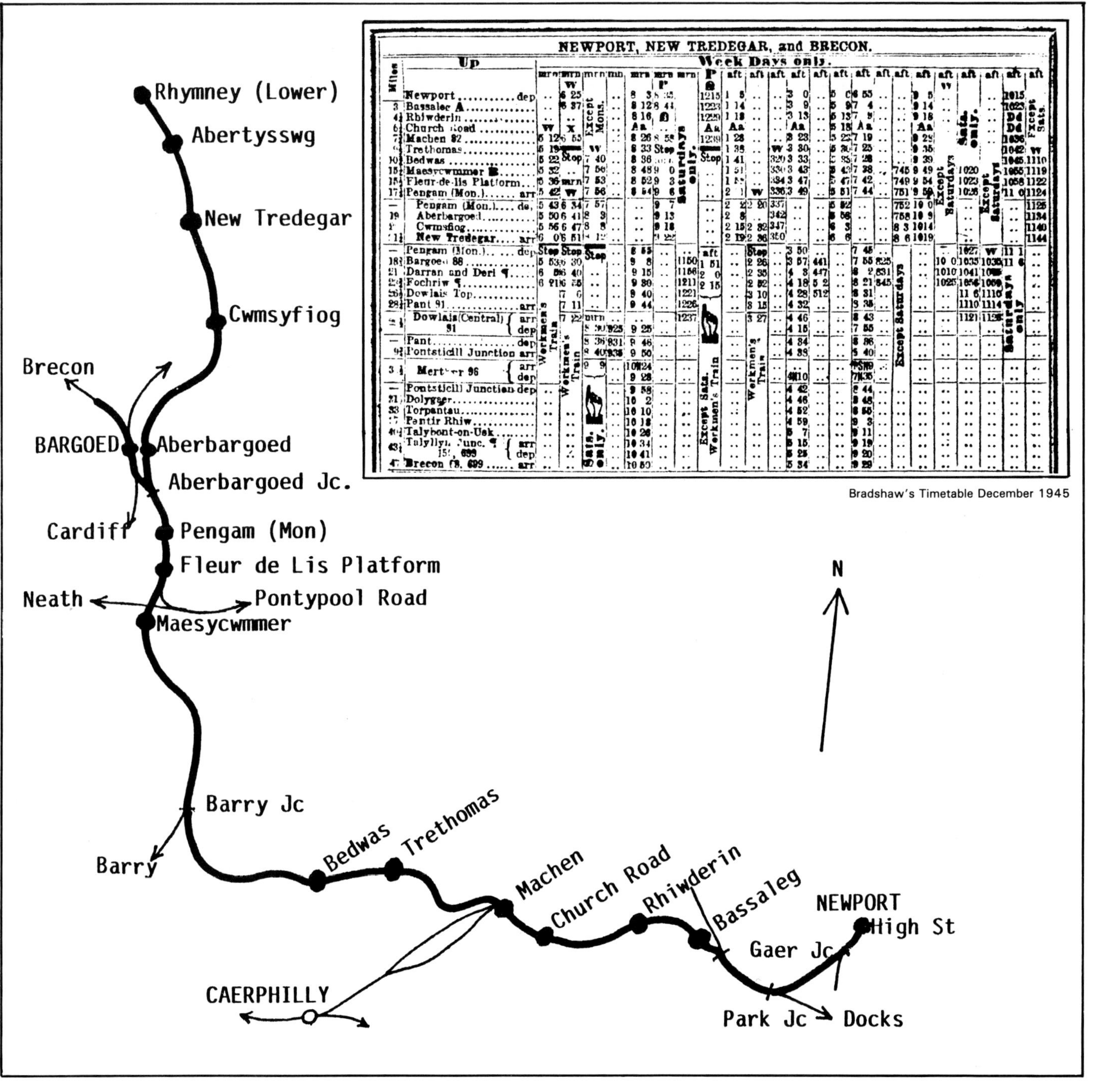

NEWPORT, NEW TREDEGAR, and BRECON.

Week Days only.

Miles	Up																				
		mrn	mrn	mrn	mrn	mrn	mrn	mrn	P	aft	aft	aft	aft	aft	aft	aft	aft	aft	aft	aft
	Newport....dep		6 25			8 38	8 35		1215	1 5			3 0		5 0	6 55			9 5		1015
3	Bassaleg A....dep		6 37			8 12	8 41		1223	1 14			3 9		5 9	7 4			9 14		1023
4½	Rhiwderin....					8 16			1229	1 19			3 13		5 13	7 9			9 18		
6	Church Road....	W	X			Aa			Aa	Aa			Aa		5 18	Aa			Aa		
7½	Machen 82....	5 12	6 55			8 26	8 55		1239	1 28			3 23		5 22	7 19			9 29		
9	Trethomas....	5 19				8 33	Stop			1 35		W	3 30		5 30	7 25			9 35		
10½	Bedwas....	5 22	Stop	7 40		8 36			Stop	1 41		3 30	3 33		5 35	7 28			9 39		
15	Maesycwmmer B....	5 32		7 50		8 48	9 0			1 51		3 30	3 43		5 43	7 38		745	9 49	1020	1055	1119
16½	Fleur-de-lis Platform....	5 36	mrn	7 53		8 52	9 3			1 55		3 34	3 47		5 47	7 42		749	9 54	1023	1058	1122
17½	Pengam (Mon.)....arr	5 42	W	7 56		8 54	9 6			2 1	W	3 36	3 49		5 51	7 44		751	9 59	1035	11 0	1124
—	Pengam (Mon.)....dep	5 43	6 34	7 57			9 7			2 22	2 20	3 37			5 52			752	10 0			1125
19	Aberbargoed....	5 50	6 41	8 3			9 13			2 8		3 42			5 58			758	10 9			1134
20	Cwmsyfiog....	5 56	6 47	8 8			9 18			2 15	2 32	3 47			6 3			8 3	1014			1140
21½	New Tredegar....arr	6 0	6 51	8 12			9 22			2 19	2 36	3 50			6 6			8 6	1019			1144
—	Pengam (Mon.)....dep	Stop	Stop	Stop		8 55			aft		Stop		3 50		7 45				1027		11 1	
18½	Bargoed 88	5 53	6 30			9 8		1150	1 51		2 26		3 57	441	7 55	8 25			10 0	1035	1036	11 6
21	Darran and Deri ¶	6 5	6 40			9 15		1156	2 0		2 35		4 3	447	8 2	8 31			1010	1041	1043	
24	Fochriw ¶	6 9	16 55			9 30		1211	2 15		2 52		4 18	5 2	8 21	845			1025	1056	1059	
26	Dowlais Top		7 6			9 40		1221			3 10		4 28	512	8 31				11 6	1110		
28½	Pant 91		7 11			9 44		1226			3 15		4 32		8 35				1110	1114		
—	Dowlais (Central) 91 {arr		7 22	mrn				1237			3 27		4 46		8 43				1121	1125		
	{dep			8 30	9 25	9 25							4 15		7 55							
—	Pant....dep			8 36	8 31	9 46							4 34		8 36							
9½	Pontsticill Junction....arr			8 40	8 35	9 50							4 39		8 40							
34	Merthyr 96 {arr			9 9		1024																
	{dep			9 28									4110		7135							
—	Pontsticill Junction....dep			9 58									4 42		8 44							
31	Dolygaer			10 2									4 46		8 45							
33	Torpantau			10 10									4 52		8 55							
37	Pentir Rhiw			10 18									4 59		9 3							
40	Talybont-on-Usk			10 26									5 7		9 11							
43½	Talyllyn Junc. ¶ {arr			10 34									5 15		9 19							
	15½, 699 {dep			10 41									5 25		9 20							
47	Brecon 8, 699....arr			10 50									5 34		9 29							

Bradshaw's Timetable December 1945

ABOVE: Maesycwmmer station on the B&M line to Newport looking up the Rhymney Valley towards Pengam. A lucky moment for the photographer as three mineral trains meet at Hengoed Viaduct where the Pontypool Road-Neath line of the GWR is carried over the B&M. In this picture of 17 March 1962 a GWR 5600 Class 0-6-2T heading for Pontypool Road is about to pass an Aberdare train from the opposite direction hauled by a 2800 Class 2-8-0. Squeezing through the arch specially built on the skew to accomodate a curve in the B&M line is a GWR 4200 Class 2-8-0T on a down mineral train for Newport. *Photo: E. R. Mountford*

New Tredegar-Newport

OPPOSITE, TOP LEFT: Down the widening Rhymney Valley, the Brecon & Merthyr line clung to its hillside shelf on the way to Bassaleg, swinging eastwards to Bedwas and Trethomas and into fairer country. The B&M became a country railway again, sharply curving as befits a line built on the course of a valley tramroad. The site of Machen station was typical of the line. It was tight, small scale, and dominated by a mountain. The down side shelter would delight a railway modeller; it was wooden and countrified with a stone end-wall, barge boarding and enamelled signs for VIROL, and there was time to admire it if you'd come from Pontypridd by way of the Caerphilly Branch. In this picture of Machen, taken in 1954, auto-fitted GWR 0-6-0PT 6402 is propelling its trailers over the crossover from the down road to the up, ready for a departure for Caerphilly and Pontypridd. *Photo: Rev R. W. A. Jones*

TOP RIGHT: Not far to go for GWR Collett 0-6-0 2218 with a Brecon-Newport train at Park Junction, Newport on 30 July 1960. The train is using the Park Junction-Gaer Junction connection to reach journey's end at Newport High Street. Brecon & Merthyr Railway ownership ended at Bassaleg in pre-grouping days and this part of the journey was by courtesy of running powers over the GWR. *Photo: Michael Hale*

RIGHT: Rural setting for a freight train between Machen and Church Road in September 1964 as GWR 2-8-0T 5210 runs bunker first down the valley in the time-honoured way of South Wales tank engines. Further contraction in the coal industry in the 1980s has led to a number of line closures in the region. Bedwas Colliery and Bedwas Coke Works (British Benzol) have ended production and the last rail movements out of Bedwas were recorded on 2 May 1986. Thanks to endowments of Carboniferous limestone at Machen a last fragment of the Brecon & Merthyr line is still alive and kicking — from Bassaleg to Powell Duffryn's Machen Quarry which supplies British Rail with 6,000 tons of ballast each week. *Photo: B. J. Ashworth*

Penygraig Branch

According to the dates on old tickets in my collection, I must have visited Llantrisant a number of times in wartime schooldays, taking a Swansea stopping train from Cardiff General or Ely Main Line. To a branch line enthusiast the attractions of 'LTS' were obvious and irresistible — three branch line trains in the bays which might be in the charge of any combination of 1471 and the two Llantrisant Metro tanks 3586 and 3594. Sometimes, luxury of luxuries, there was AEC railcar No.22 waiting to go to Cowbridge.

Llantrisant station retained some of its stone built elegance in spite of GWR extensions. I write in the past tense because it is long gone, having been closed by the WR on 2 November 1964.

A wartime memory is the "Is Your Journey Really Necessary?" notice over the booking office window and the wall display with the hand written alphabetical list of revised fares — revised upwards — of course! One of the longest nameboards I had ever seen stood at the western end of the up platform:

"LLANTRISANT Change for TONYREFAIL and PENYGRAIG Cowbridge and Taff Vale line"

RIGHT: The scene at Llantrisant station looking east towards Cardiff on the South Wales main line in September 1954. A Cardiff-Bridgend return football excursion calls with GWR 2-6-2T 3100 of Tondu shed in charge. Waiting in the bay on the left is Llantrisant's GWR 0-4-2T 1471 with the connecting one coach auto train for Penygraig. Until 1952 the Pontypridd auto also left from this bay. The Cowbridge trains left from the outer face of the down platform which is behind the main line train.
Photo: Rev R. W. A. Jones

ORIGIN:	**Ely Valley Railway**
	Ely & Clydach Valleys Railway
LENGTH	**9m 28ch**
OPENED:	**December 1862 (Freight: Llantrisant-Penygraig)**
	August 1878 (Freight: Penygraig-Clydach Vale)
	1 May 1901 (Passenger: Llantrisant-Penygraig)
CLOSED:	**9 June 1958 (Passenger: Llantrisant-Penygraig)**
	3 April 1967 (Freight: Coed Ely-Clydach Vale)
	30 November 1983 (Freight: Mwyndy Junction-Coed Ely)
RULING GRADIENT:	**1 in 40**

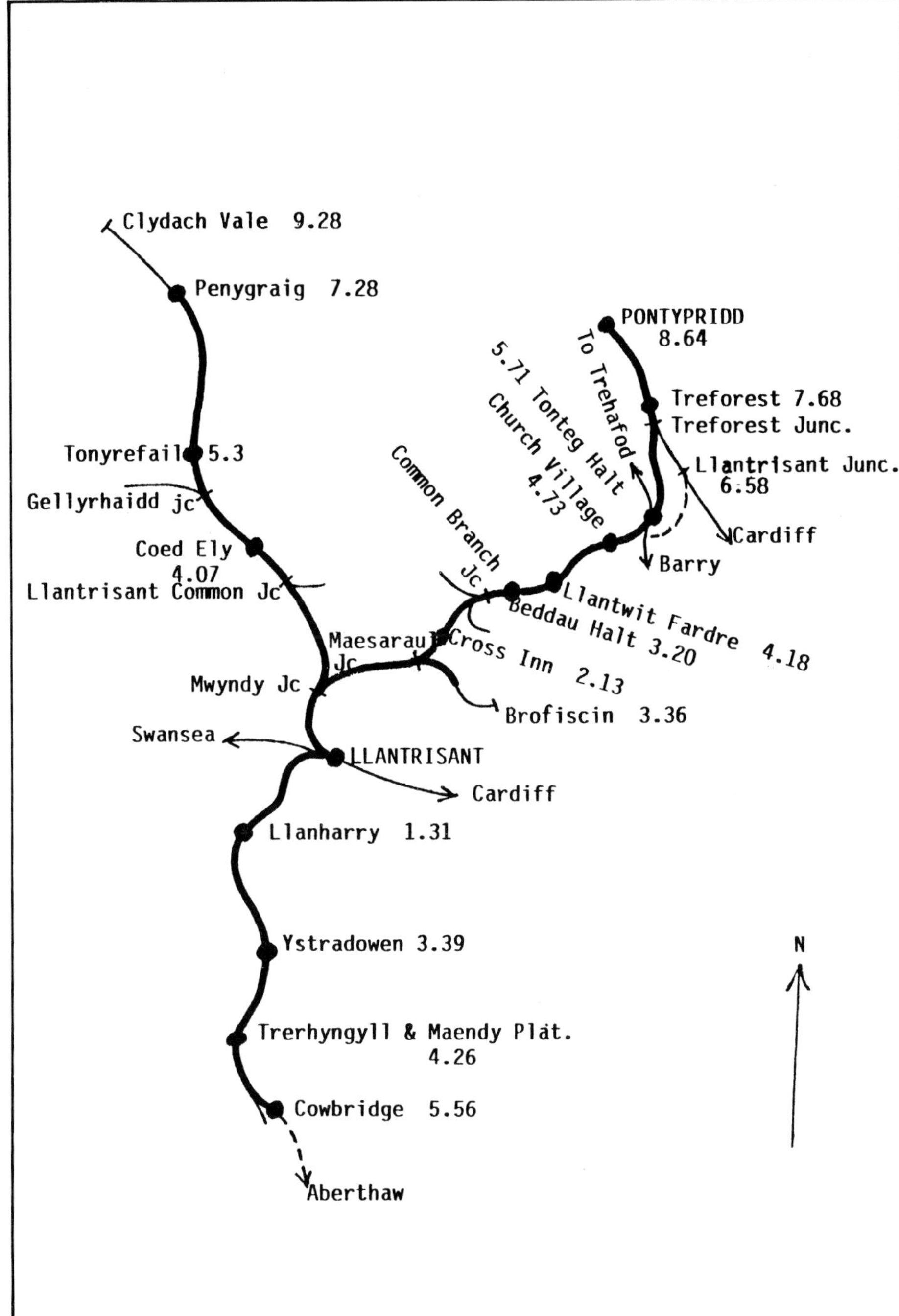

The opening of the broad gauge South Wales Railway between Chepstow and Swansea on 18 June 1850 stimulated the exploitation of iron ore and coal resources in the Llantrisant region. Incorporated in 1857, the broad gauge Ely Valley Railway opened mineral lines from Llantrisant to Mwyndy and Brofiscin (1859) and to Penygraig (1862) with a branch to Gellyrhaidd (later extended to Gilfach Goch). The Ely Valley lines were leased to the GWR in 1861 but the inconvenience of the broad gauge in South Wales lasted until 1872.

The journey up the Ely Valley was a pleasantly rural experience with pastoral and occasional woodland scenery predominating over industry as far as Tonyrefail. From there on the prospect was bleaker and more alpine as the up and down lines rose on divided gradients to ease the way to the summit. Tonyrefail and Penygraig were the two original stations on this double track branch, both with the usual facilities for goods. Coed Ely, with sectional concrete type platforms and buildings, was commissioned in 1925 to serve the mining village. Electric lighting penetrated the branch as far as Tonyrefail station; Penygraig alone stayed gaslit until the end.

Metro 2-4-0 tanks 3586 and 3594 were much in evidence on the line in wartime when I remember a make-up of two GWR 'matchboard' ex steam railcar trailers on the auto trains. At that time as many as 14 daily passenger trains competed for space with the many coal trains hauled by pannier tanks and 2-8-0 tanks of the 4200 series. Daily trains from Penygraig took war workers to Tremains Platform for the ordnance factory east of Bridgend. After the war the inevitable road competition resumed and there were only four trains each way and two more on Saturdays when the passenger service ended on 9 June 1958. The well loved branch mainstay, number 1471, which came new to Llantrisant in 1936, was then sent to the greener pastures of the Exe Valley in Devon.

Coal traffic on the branch had disappeared north of Coed Ely by 1967 and the section was closed. The Coed Ely Coke plant, last customer of the railway, ended production in 1983 and Mwyndy Junction-Coed Ely closed on 30 November that year. The last remnant of the Ely Valley lines to go was Llantrisant-Cwm Llantwit, on 2 March 1987, when a final mineral train used the line to Cwm — a sad end indeed to a long partnership between the railway and the coalfield. Before the track was lifted, a railtour train ran between Llantrisant and Cwm on 11th April 1987.

ABOVE: Rhondda townscape from the footbridge at Penygraig station, looking towards Llantrisant in September 1954. On the horizon is the watershed between the rivers Rhondda and Ely over which the branch train has climbed at 1 in 40 from Cilely Siding. GWR 0-4-2T 1471, the regular performer on the Ely Valley Branch in the 1950s, drifts into Penygraig with the auto from Llantrisant. The afternoon sun picks out the waste tips of Naval Colliery while Mynydd Dinas dominates the mining community of Williamstown. *Photo: Rev R. W. A. Jones*

Table 133   LLANTRISANT and PENYGRAIG—(Third class only)

Week Days only

Miles		a.m	a.m	a.m	a.m	p.m	p.m	p.m	p.m	p.m	p.m S	p.m	p.m S	p.m S
	Llantrisant.... dep	7 5	8 18	9 25	11 10	12 45	1 40	3 55	4 45	5 40	6 55	7 55	9 13	9 55
4	Coed Ely	7 15	8 29	9 35	11 20	12 55	1 50	4 5	4 55	5 50	7 5	8 5	9 23	10 5
5	Tonyrefail	7 25	8 37	9 40	11 25	1 0	1 55	4 10	5 0	5 55	7 10	8 10	9 28	10 10
7¾	Penygraig ■ .... arr	7 33	8 44	9 47	11 32	1 7	2 2	4 17	5 7	6 2	7 17	8 17	9 35	10 17

Week Days only

Miles		a.m	a.m	a.m	p.m	p.m	p.m	p.m	p.m	p.m	p.m S	p.m	p.m S	p.m S
	Penygraig .... dep	7 50	8 46	10 25	12 10	1 10	2 55	4 24	5 10	6 30	7 20	8 30	9 37	10 20
2½	Tonyrefail	7 55	8 51	10 30	12 15	1 15	3 0	4 29	5 15	6 35	7 25	8 35	9 42	10 25
3½	Coed Ely	7 58	8 54	10 33	12 18	1 18	3 3	4 32	5 19	6 38	7 28	8 38	9 45	10 29
7½	Llantrisant .... arr	8 6	9 2	10 41	12 26	1 26	3 11	4 40	5 26	6 46	7 35	8 46	9 53	10 36

■ Nearly 1 mile to Dinas (Rhondda) Station.   S Saturdays only.

WR Timetable No.133 25 September 1950

Penygraig Branch

RIGHT: The GWR look prevails at Tonyrefail on 31 May 1958 as 1471, in charge of the 4.55 pm from Llantrisant to Penygraig, calls to set down an elderly shopper. The porter's chair, extreme left, indicates a quiet afternoon's duty in the sun. *Photo: Ian L. Wright*

BELOW: Two 0-6-0 pannier tanks, No.4637 leading, with a sandwich of brake vans, take turns for water at the arrival platform at Penygraig on 15 February 1958. From here, the line continued for two miles to serve collieries at Clydach Vale. *Photo: Hugh Davies*

Cowbridge Branch

The Cowbridge Branch was most people's idea of what a rural railway byway ought to be. A line where life seemed to run at a leisurely pace; where the branch train was old, often incredibly old, and you got the impression as you stepped off the train at Cowbridge, (more often than not the only passenger), that people were of less importance than coal, cattle feed and the Hereford steers being dealt with in the nearby goods yard. As far as really old trains go it would be hard to beat the day in 1947 when 2-4-0T 3586 turned up at Cowbridge hauling clerestory-roofed auto coach No.35, converted from a unit of the Cornishman in 1904.

Although the Cowbridge line looked like a Great Western branch it was in fact a detached outpost of the Taff Vale Railway, its real focus being standard gauge Pontypridd rather than broad gauge Llantrisant. Cowbridge, the quiet market town for the rural Vale of Glamorgan, had been by-passed by the South Wales Railway 5½ miles to the north and in 1862 the Cowbridge Railway was incorporated to build a standard gauge branch to the Llantrisant & TV Junction Railway at Maesaraul. The TVR agreed to work the line which opened for traffic in 1865, a third rail being used between Llantrisant and Maesaraul by agreement with the GWR.

Between 1905 and 1913 the TVR was using steam railcars on the line with a through service from Pontypridd to Cowbridge and Aberthaw to which the Cowbridge line had been extended in 1892. Although the TVR had used auto trains on the branch it was not until 1930 that the GWR did so, and from 1930 the Cowbridge and Pontypridd services became two separate branch services running to and from Llantrisant with improved connections to GWR stations.

The Cowbridge Branch had an almost totally rural environment with steep gradients, sharp curves and undulating course and the Taff Vale's miniature single track timber overline bridges were particularly delightful. The branch was single, and excepting Cowbridge Junction loop, there were no intermediate crossing loops or signals, Llanharry and Ystradowen stations being merely single platforms and the various siding connections were all controlled from ground frames.

ORIGIN:	Cowbridge Railway (Taff Vale Railway)
LENGTH:	5m 56ch
OPENED:	30 January 1865 (Freight) 18 September 1865 (Passenger)
CLOSED:	26 November 1951 (Passenger: Llantrisant-Cowbridge)
	1 February 1965 (Freight: Llanharry-Cowbridge)
	31 December 1975 (Freight: Llantrisant-Llanharry)
RULING GRADIENT:	1 in 45

The Cowbridge & Aberthaw Railway (incorporated 1889 and vested in the TVR in 1895) opened a single line extension from Cowbridge to Aberthaw on 1 October 1892. The line was closed to passengers on 5 May 1930 and for freight on 1 November 1932.

BELOW: The later Cowbridge station of 1892, seen in wartime with the first AEC railcar to be allocated to the branch, GWR No.22. I took the picture (at *some* risk of arrest) on 18 September 1943.
Photo: Ian L. Wright

LLANTRISANT AND COWBRIDGE.

Week Days only—One class only.

Miles		a.m.	a.m.	a.m.	a.m.	p.m.	p.m.	p.m.	p.m.	p.m.	p.m.	p.m. (Sats. only)
	Llantrisant . . dep.	6 46	8 20	9 20	10 55	12 50	2 20	3 55	6 0	7 55	9 35	10 35
1½	Llanharry . . . . ,,	6 49	8 24	9 24	10 59	12 54	2 24	3 59	6 4	7 59	9 39	10 39
3½	Ystradowen . . ,,	6 55	8 30	9 30	11 5	1 0	2 30	4 5	6 10	8 5	9 45	10 45
4½	Trerhyngyll and Maendy ,,	6 58	8 33	9 33	11 8	1 3	2 33	4 8	6 13	8 8	9 48	10 48
5½	Cowbridge . . arr.	7 3	8 38	9 38	11 13	1 8	2 38	4 13	6 18	8 13	9 53	10 53

	a.m.	a.m.	a.m.	p.m.	p.m.	p.m. (Weds. only)	p.m. (Sats. only)	p.m.	p.m.	p.m.	p.m. (Sats. excepted)	p.m. (Sats. only)	p.m.	p.m.	p.m.	p.m. (Sats. only)
Cowbridge . . dep.	7 18	8 42	10 3	12 22	1 15	1 25		1V38	3 22	4 30	4 55		6 38	8 48	10 8	11 0
Trerhyngyll and Maendy . . . ,,	7 22	8 46	10 7	12 26	1 19	1 29		1V42	3 26	4 34	4 59		6 42	8 52	10 12	11 4
Ystradowen . . ,,	7 26	8 50	10 11	12 30	1 23	1 33		1V46	3 30	4 38	5 3		6 46	8 56	10 16	11 8
Llanharry . . . . ,,	7 31	8 55	10 16	12 35	1 28	1 38		1V51	3 35	4 43	5 8		6 51	9 1	10 21	11 13
Llantrisant . . arr.	7 36	9 0	10 21	12 40	1 34	1 43		1V56	3 40	4 48	5 13		6 56	9 6	10 26	11 18

GWR Passenger Timetable 3 July 1939

ABOVE: Iron ore at Llanharry. GWR 0-6-0PT 3644 is propelling a train of loaded iron ore hoppers the 1½ miles from Llanharry Iron Ore Mine siding to Llantrisant on 22 February 1963. The closed Llanharry passenger platform is in the foreground and the mine headgear can be seen behind the engine. The remunerative iron ore traffic kept active until 1975 with English Electric Type 3 Co Co diesels working to Llanharry for a number of years, to be followed by trips with the Llantrisant Class 08 yard shunter. *Photo: Ron Mason*

LEFT: The train shed of the original passenger terminus at Eastgate Street, Cowbridge, in August 1957. To the right are the cattle pens and goods shed. *Photo: Ian L. Wright*

Llantrisant-Pontypridd

LLANTRISANT BRANCH

ORIGIN:	**Ely Valley Railway**
	LLantrisant & Taff Vale Junction Railway
	Taff Vale Railway
LENGTH:	**6m 58ch Llantrisant-Llantrisant Junction (Treforest)**
OPENED:	**1 December 1863 (Freight: Llantrisant Junction (Treforest)-Maesaraul Junction)**
	8 February 1865 (Freight: Maesaraul Junction-Llantrisant-Cowbridge)
	18 September 1865 (Passenger: Llantrisant Junction (Treforest)-Llantrisant-Cowbridge)
CLOSED:	**31 March 1952 (Passenger: Llantrisant-Pontypridd)**
	7 September 1963 (Freight: Treforest Junction-Maesaraul Junction — Local Goods)
	28 September 1964 (Freight: Treforest Junction-Cwm Colliery Siding)
	2 March 1987 (Freight: Llantrisant-Cwm Colliery — last mineral train ran)
RULING GRADIENT:	**1 in 40**

BROFISCIN BRANCH

ORIGIN:	**Ely Valley Railway (Mwyndy Branch)**
LENGTH:	**1m 72ch Maesaraul Junction-Brofiscin**
OPENED:	**February 1859**
CLOSED:	**Pre 1936 (Mwyndy Siding-Brofiscin)**
	7 November 1968 (Maesaraul Junction-Mwyndy Siding)
RULING GRADIENT:	**1 in 120**

In 1859 the broad gauge Ely Valley Railway built a mineral branch north and eastwards from Llantrisant station to iron ore mines being developed at Mwyndy, south east of the old hill town of Llantrisant, and opened it as a horse worked line. It followed the Afon Clun to Maesaraul where it turned south eastwards to serve the Bute and Mwyndy mines which between them produced 400,000 tons of high quality haematite ore in the boom years 1870-75. Closed in the 1880s because of foreign competition, the mines are now lost and forgotten. It was a secret, overgrown line beyond Mwyndy Siding where there was a coal yard and an ICI gunpowder enclosure. The branch continued its rural windings into the Glamorgan countryside and ended among farms at Brofiscin. The track beyond Mwyndy Siding was lifted in 1936.

A sequel to this encounter was an invitation to join the crew for a ride on the loco the rest of the way down the branch. Better still was to follow. "We're going down to Cowbridge Yard to pick up a loaded cattle wagon. Want to ride with us?" Clearly this was an offer we could not (and did not) refuse! It was an example of the friendliness of the country railwayman and the relaxed approach to affairs on Welsh railway byways in the 1950s.

RIGHT: The shunter of a train on the Brofiscin (Mwyndy) Branch holds the gates for GWR 0-6-0PT 9780 to pass Maesaraul Crossing on its way from Llantrisant to Mwyndy Siding in August 1957. The original crossing keeper's house is on the right.

Photo: Ian L. Wright

RIGHT: There were three stations on the Llantrisant Branch, at Cross Inn, Llantwit Fardre and Church Village. All were single platform affairs, the first two having small goods yards, but Church Village, added to the railway map in 1887, was never provided with goods facilities of any kind. It became an unstaffed halt as a result of economies in 1932. Llantwit Fardre station was the earliest building, a stone structure with hipped roof, which opened to passengers in 1867. Its staff pose in the sun for this photograph of about 1900. *Photo: Colin Chapman Collection*

LEFT: Climbing to Llantwit from both directions with gradients at each end as steep as 1 in 40, the Llantrisant Branch was quite a difficult line to work. It was single from Cowbridge Road Crossing to Tonteg Junction and worked by electric train staff with crossing loops at Llantwit and at Common Branch Junction where lines went off to Llantrisant Common and southeastward to Waterhall Junction. GWR 'Metro' 2-4-0T 3586, the last of its class to work in South Wales, emerges from a woodland setting at Llantwit Fardre in May 1948 with an ex GWR steam car driving trailer forming an auto train for Pontypridd. Needless to say, travel over this branch was 30 minutes of sheer delight especially if you could persuade your driver to let you ride in the front of the trailer on the way back! *Photo: Ian L. Wright*

Up Trains.   LLANTRISANT AND PONTYPRIDD (CENTRAL).   Week Days only.

Mile Post Mileage from Maesaraul Jct. (M.)	(C.)	Distance (M.)	(C.)	STATIONS	Station No.	Gradient 1 in	Express Trains Point to Point Times	Allow for Stop	Allow for Start	Ordinary Trains Point to Point Times	Allow for Stop	Allow for Start
.	—	—	—	**Llantrisant** ..	2720	379 R	—	—	1	—	—	1
—	—	0	61	Cowbridge Rd.Cg.	2745	L	—	—	—	—	—	—
—	—	1	37	Maesaraul Junct.	2746	100 R	3	1	2	6	1	3
0	23	1	60	Cottage Siding	—	40 R	—	—	—	—	—	—
0	51	2	8	**Cross Inn** ..	7573	50 R	—	—	—	6	1	2
1	16	2	53	Common Br'ch Jc.	7744	50 R	—	—	—	6	1	2
1	59	3	15	Beddau Halt ..	7644	L	—	—	—	—	—	—
2	0	3	37	Cwm Colliery Jo.	7748	2 0 R	—	—	—	4	1	1
2	59	4	16	**Llantwit** ..	7592	L	8	1	1	3	1	1
3	32	4	69	**Church Village**	7568	264 F	—	—	—	—	—	—
4	35	5	72	Tonteg Halt ..	7672	40 F	—	—	—	—	—	—
—	—	—	—	Stop Board	—	—	—	—	—	—	—	—
5	21	6	5	Llantrisant Jo....	7866	223 R	15	1	—	18	1	—

Time allowances for Freight Trains.

STATIONS	K 8.20 a.m. Pen'th Curve Empties arr.	dep.	B Pontypridd (Central) Passenger arr.	dep.	B Pontypridd (Central) Passenger arr.	dep.	F Pfaldcaiach Iron Ore arr.	dep.	B Pontypridd (Central) Passenger arr.	dep.	K Coke Ovens Goods arr.	dep.		B Pontypridd (Central) Passenger arr.	dep.
Llantrisant ..	..	..	—	**7 15**	—	**7 53**	—	7 55	—	**8 30**	—	10 5	..	—	**10 30**
Cowbridge Rd.Cg.	R	R	C 7 16 S		O 7 56 S		C S		C 8 33 S		C S		....	O 10 33 S	
Maesaraul Junct.	..	..	C S		C S		C S		C S		C S		..	O S	
Cottage Siding	....	...	—		—		—		—		—		....	—	
Cross Inn ..	..	..	—	7 22	—	8 0	—	—	—	8 37	S T		..	—	10 37
Common Br'ch Jc.	9 6		7 24 X	7 27	C S		8	8	C S		10 24 X	10 30	....	C S	
Beddau Halt ..	—		—	7 30	—	8 4	—		—	8 41	—		..	—	10 41
Cwm Colliery Jo.	9 11	—	—		—		—		—		—		..	—	
Llantwit ..			7 33 X	7 34	8 7	8 8	8 16 X	9 0	8 44 X	8 50	10 40	11 0	..	10 44	10 45
Church Village	SUS-		—	7 37	—	8 11	—		—	8 52	—		....	—	10 48
Tonteg Halt ..	PEN-		—	7 41	—	8 15	—		—	8 56	—		....	—	10 52
Stop Board	DED.		—		—		P		—		P		....	—	
Llantrisant Jo....	.. H 2		C 7 44 S		C 8 18 S		9 25	9 30	C 8 59 S		11 25	11 50	..	C 10 55 S	

Footer route codes: B   K   B   K   K   B   K   K   B   B   F   B   K   B   (Z 3)   (X 2)

GWR Service Timetable No.9 September 1928

The pleasant south facing Pennant Sandstone country lying between Llantrisant and the Taff Valley had long been exploited for coal, but on a small scale along the coalfield's southern outcrop. As early as 1697 Llantwit Fardre had "Coale works very numerous in most grounds in the parish" to quote a writer of nearly three centuries ago. Backed by the upland slopes of Mynydd y Glyn, the rural village of Llantwit Fardre was set among hill farms but with the development of coal mining around Llantwit in the 19th century, new settlements grew up along the Llantrisant road, at Tonteg, Church Village and Newtown Llantwit.

The Taff Vale Railway, through its subsidiary the Llantrisant & Taff Vale Junction Railway, built a single line branch from Llantrisant Junction (Treforest) to meet the EVR Mwyndy Branch at Maesaraul and opened it for goods traffic in 1863, the EVR granting the L&TVJR powers to run over the Mwyndy Branch and agreeing to lay a third rail. The TVR's object was to reach the Llantwit collieries and to establish a shorter standard gauge route between the Mwyndy iron ore field and Dowlais. Iron ore for Merthyr and Dowlais could now be hauled 19 miles by the L&TVJ route as compared with the incredible 54 miles it took by the broad gauge route

via Neath. The GWR had come into the picture in 1861 by leasing the EVR. Eventually an arrangement was made with the GWR and the Cowbridge Railway (which the TVR had agreed to work) and a third rail was laid between Maesaraul and Llantrisant station. This enabled the TVR to put on a through passenger service between Pontypridd, Llantrisant and Cowbridge on 18 September 1865, a pattern which was to remain until 1930 when the GWR began working the lines as two separate branches.

Coal was by far the most important commodity carried over the lines of the Taff Vale system and it was good news for the Western Region in 1951 when

Llantrisant-Pontypridd

the National Coal Board decided on heavy investment in Cwm Llantwit Colliery which had been served by the Llantrisant Branch since 1912.

In 1930 the GWR decided to rationalise the railways at Tonteg. A new connection was made to the ex Barry Railway Treforest Branch at Tonteg Junction which eased the descent to Treforest to 1 in 101 and the old TVR 1 in 40 incline to Treforest was abandoned. Coal traffic from Cwm continued to pass down to Treforest until 1964 when more rationalisation took place. Cwm-Treforest Junction was closed from 28 September 1964 and the flow of traffic was reversed. Access to Cwm was now to be via the South Wales main line, Llantrisant and Mwyndy Junction.

The decline in demand for coal has brought closure and redundancy to even the most modern of South Wales mines with catastrophic effect on the railway. In 1986 it was announced that Cwm Llantwit would close. The roar of Llantrisant's Class 37 diesels through Cross Inn is already a thing of the past, and this last of the Llantrisant byways closed down on 2 March 1987.

LEFT: GWR 0-6-2T 5630, one of a class of 200 built for mixed traffic work in South Wales, brings a train of coal and coke from Cwm down the 1930 connection to Tonteg Junction and the Treforest Branch in February 1958. Tonteg Halt, built new by the GWR in 1930, is on the left of the picture. In the foreground is the double track ex Barry Railway main line with the down platform of Tonteg Halt, looking towards the Garth Hill and Efail Isaf. *Photo: Derek Chaplin*

RIGHT, TOP: Veteran GWR 'Metro' 2-4-0T 3594 of Llantrisant shed idles some time away on the spare road at Pontypridd station with auto trailer 106 on 14 August 1946. Note her brass numberplate, GWR monogram and the letters LTS on the front of her frame. *Photo: Ian L. Wright*

RIGHT: Pure Taff Vale! GWR 397, a TVR A Class 0-6-2T leaves Tonteg Halt with a late afternoon Pontypridd-Llantrisant train on 5 June 1948. The coaches are a pair of converted TV steam car trailers being worked non-auto, as the Class A tanks were not auto fitted. The passenger service, which served another halt, at Beddau, was withdrawn in 1952 after 30 years of intense local bus competition.*Photo: Ian L. Wright*

Cardiff-Rhydyfelin

I came to live in Cardiff as a small boy in 1932. Ours was a Birchgrove address but we lived at the wrong end of Caerphilly Road for my parents to have much to do with Birchgrove Halt and the trains on the Coryton Branch. It was a long road and they preferred the No.28 bus.

The Coryton line is remarkable for its changes of fortune which continue down to the present day. The Bute Docks Co., with the Barry Railway's success possibly in mind, decided to become a dock owning railway company so that Rhondda coal could be conveyed by its own railway to its own port of Cardiff. Incorporated as the Cardiff Railway in 1897, the Company built an ill-fated double track main line at huge expense. Only one train ever ran over the whole length of the line — on 15 May 1909 — when a ceremonial coal train crossed Rhydyfelin Viaduct with the Marquis of Bute on board. In 1911 the CR formally opened the line, from Heath Junction (Rhymney Railway) to Rhydyfelin, but it failed to out-manoeuvre the opposition of the Taff Vale Railway to a CR junction at Treforest. Unable to get hold of the coal traffic for which it was built, the railway fell on hard times and was closed by the GWR beyond Coryton in 1931. The GWR however, did not remove the track.

The remainder of the CR survived as the Coryton Branch and Cardiff's suburbs expanded northwards to meet it.

For years on end, from the 1960s, the Coryton DMU trains were under constant threat of closure. In 1987 came change of fortune again as the Coryton Branch became part of the City Line cross-city service between Coryton and Radyr, and a new halt was opened at Ty Glas.

ORIGIN:	Cardiff Railway
LENGTH:	8m 48ch Heath Junction-Rhydyfelin halt
OPENED:	1 March 1911 (Passenger & Freight)
CLOSED:	20 July 1931 (Passenger & Freight: Rhydyfelin halt-Coryton halt)
RE-OPENED:	28 August 1951 (Freight: Nantgarw Colliery-Coryton)
CLOSED:	16 June 1952 (Freight: Glanyllyn-Coryton)
NEW SPUR OPENED:	16 June 1952 (Freight: Taffs Well-Glanyllyn) The Taffs Well-Nantgarw Colliery Branch has been out of use since 8 January 1987 pending closure.
RULING GRADIENT:	1 in 75 (1 in 50 from 19 November 1984)

RIGHT: Heath Junction, where the Coryton Branch diverged from the ex Rhymney line two miles north of Cardiff Queen Street. A Coryton-Cardiff Queen Street auto train propelled by a GWR 4500 Class Prairie tank is joining the former RR main line during snowy conditions in March 1956. *Photo: Derek Chaplin*

The price of Coryton Branch survival in the modern commercial world, this opulent junction and manual signal box disappeared in 1984 and the land was sold for housing. 14 chains further north the Coryton Sprinter DMUs take a more basic turnout into the birch trees, diving down at 1 in 50 to regain the original trackbed. Electronic control of the branch is from a new ground level Heath Junction cabin on the down side of the RR line.

ABOVE: Whitchurch (Glam) station building, photographed in 1956. This neat red brick structure was on the up (Coryton bound) side with a waiting room, booking office and platform awning. An iron footbridge linked the up and down platforms which were laid out on a generous scale. With goods yard, goods shed and original CR signalbox, Whitchurch had great charm and epitomised the rural railway station. Demolition of the station and sale of the land to developers has had tragic visual consequences. Waiting patrons of BR gaze daily at a sordid row of backs of garages built on to the up platform edge. *Photo: Derek Chaplin*

BELOW: Close up of TV driving trailer W2507W on 13 July 1957 at Coryton Halt, the terminus to which GWR trains were cut back in 1931. The TVR trailer, dating from 1907, was the leading car of a 'sandwich' auto train with a 5500 Class 2-6-2T in the middle of the 1.00 pm departure for Queen Street. *Photo: Hugh Davies*

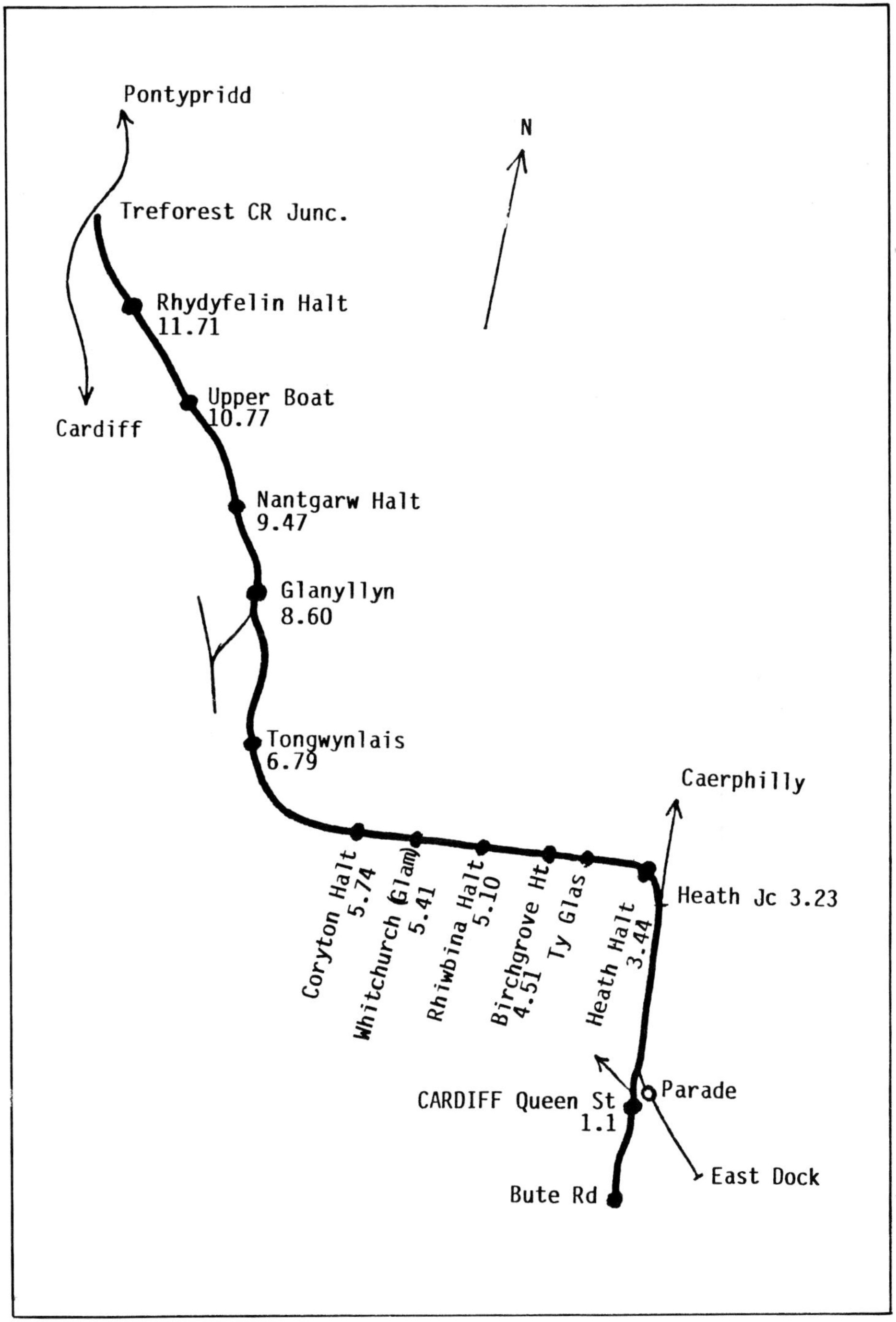

ABOVE: Until 1966 the Coryton Branch was double track with up and down platforms at Heath Halt Low Level, Birchgrove Halt, Rhiwbina Halt and Whitchurch (Glam) station. The exception was the single line between Whitchurch and Coryton where the terminal loop was controlled from a ground frame opened by key on the electric train staff which was picked up from the Whitchurch signalman. Cathays shed usually provided passenger engines for the Coryton line with Cardiff East Dock shed providing for freight. GWR 2-6-2T 4580, on a Coryton-Cardiff Queen Street auto train, waits for the Heath Halt starter to clear before moving off to join the Rhymney line at Heath Junction, one evening in 1954. *Photo: Rev R. W. A. Jones*

Cardiff-Rhydyfelin

Up Trains.

Week Days.

Distance from Wharf Road, East Cardiff Docks, also Mile Post mileage. (M)	(C)	STATIONS.	Station No.	Gradient 1 in	K Goods. arr.	K Goods. dep.	H 4.50 a.m. West M'ydef to Radyr Jcn Empties MX dep.	B Passenger. arr.	B Passenger. dep.	B Auto Passenger. arr.	B Auto Passenger. dep.	K Goods. arr.	K Goods. dep.
					A.M.	A.M.	A.M.	A.M.	A.M.	A.M.	A.M.	A.M.	A.M.
—	—	Cardiff East Docks Loco Shed	....	L	....	....	....	....	....	....	....	....	....
0	12	Roath Basin Junction	..	114 R			5 39	..	..			–	5 15
—	—	L.M.S. Yard Junction	8013	147 R	....	..	—	....	....			—	—
0	60	Tyndall Street Junction	8015	4200 R	..	..	—	..	..	..	..	—	—
—	—	Gaol Lane Sidings	8018	4200 R	..	..	—	....	....			5 22	5 30
—	—	Cardiff (Bute Road)	7565	623 R	..	..	..	..	..	..	..		..
—	—	Bute Street	7817	152 R	....	....	...			....	....		....
—	—	Cardiff (Queen Strret)	7563	750 R			..	—	5 10	—	5 25	..	..
—	—	Queen Street North	....	....	....	....	5 46	—	—	—	—	—	—
—	—	Machine Road	..	..	—	3 20	—	—	—	—	—	—	—
2	4	Crwys Sidings	8027	101 R	—	—	Y 1	--	—	—	—	5 36	5 45
2	23	Heath Junction	8-31	85 R	—	—	..	—	—	—	—	5 52	6 0
3	44	Heath Halt (Low Level)	7656	75 R	....	....	....	....	....	—	5 32	—	—
4	48	Phœnix Brick Works	..	L	..	..	..	..	..	—	—	6 6	6 16
5	10	Rhiwbina Halt	7666	L	....	....	....	....	....	5 35	5 36	—	—
5	41	Whitchurch (Glam.)	7636	L	..	..	..	..	..	5 38	5 39	6 20	8 18
5	74	Coryton Halt (Glam.)	7650	L	....	....	....	....	....	—	5 41	—	—
6	79	Tongwynlais	7624	L	..	..	..	..	..	—	5 44	8 25 S	T 8 30
—	—	Portobello Quarry	....	....	....	....	....	....	....	—	—	—	—
8	60	Glanyllyn	7584	L	..	..	..	..	..	—	5 49	8 38 S	T 8 45
9	47	Nantgarw Halt (Low Level)	7662	660 F	....	....	....	....	....	5 51	5 52	D	9
10	6	Nantgarw Colliery	..	L	..	..	..	..	..	—	—	—	—
10	77	Upper Boat	7633	200 R	....	....	....	....	....	—	5 55	8 55	9||15
11	71	Rhydyfelin Halt (Low Level)	7669	75 R			..	..	..	5 58	—	9||18	--

Extracted from GWR Service Timetable September 1928, pages 90/91

RIGHT: Waiting for customers in suburbia, 13 July 1957. Marshalled in 'sandwich' formation at Coryton Halt, where there is a single platform on the up side only, a 5500 Class Prairie tank, believed to be the preserved 5572, has arrived with the 12.10 pm auto train from Cardiff Bute Road. Gas lighting and pagoda shelters are the order of the day. *Photo: Hugh Davies*

BELOW: One of the original Cardiff Railway steam railcars at the track level terminal halt in 1911. At that period there was a signalbox, run round loop, water tank and coal stage. The track level shelter and gated enclosure (unlocked by the conductor-guard who leans against the buffer) can be seen between the railcar and the box. *Photo: Pontypridd Central Library*

In Cardiff Railway days the passenger service to Rhydyfelin was worked by a steam railcar and trailer of which the CR had two sets. Trains ran to and from the Rhymney Railway station at Cardiff (Parade), the first part of the route to Heath Junction being run over two miles of the RR main line. The GWR closed Parade station in 1928 and all RR and CR line trains used an enlarged Cardiff Queen Street station with some CR line trains being extended to Cardiff Bute Road.

Between 1922 and 1931 the GWR put on an unbelievable variety of non-standard South Wales locomotive types and coaching miscellanea to work the Rhydyfelin trains. In the post war years after 1945 some of this variety still survived in the two sets of peak hour trains used between Bute Road and Coryton. At off peak times a Cathays 6400 Class 0-6-0PT worked auto with a pair of Taff Vale or Cardiff Railway trailers.

RIGHT: GWR ex TV Class A 0-6-2T 376 has just run round her train on the Coryton loop on 14 February 1948, ready for the return to Bute Road. The three high roofed vehicles in the train are TV bogie thirds of 1921. The second car is a TV railmotor trailer and the third a Rhymney brake third. With nearly 40 years of advancing tree growth at Coryton the site presents a very different picture today. *Photo: Ian L. Wright*

The opening under the road bridge at Coryton is no longer the gateway to a mysterious line beyond. In 1986, arriving on the DMU from Cardiff, I found it summarily boarded up with sleepers. In the Great Western's official book the branch to Rhydyfelin had been closed beyond Coryton on 20 July 1931, but through the bridge the track curved into a deep cutting and as year succeeded year the line took on the look of a nature reserve, complete with three abandoned stations, a quarry siding and a tunnel. It was a nature trail that still saw occasional trains as I discovered one day in September 1939 when I met GWR 73 waiting in the cutting with a short goods train. The Rhymney 0-6-2 tank had been up the branch to Nantgarw Colliery on some errand for the Powell Duffryn Company. Her crew were on the ballast waiting for the traffic man to walk back from Whitchurch box carrying the staff for closing the catch points and the key for unlocking the Coryton ground frame.

LEFT: GWR rebuilt 0-6-2T 155, the only Cardiff Railway engine of its class of Kitsons still working on the GWR, stands in Coryton Cutting waiting for the ground frame key after returning with empties from the NCB site at Nantgarw. I have reason to remember the date, 4 September 1948, because I had been up to Nantgarw and back with Driver Britton on the footplate. *Photo: Ian L. Wright*

Cardiff-Rhydyfelin

Few places in Wales appealed to me more than the square mile of country to the south of Taff's Well. It is an area of dramatic contrasts in land forms where natural beauty, modified by the works of man, is combined with the remains of an industrial past. Through the wooded Garth Gap where the River Taff has carved a limestone gorge, the Cardiff Railway squeezed below the rock face in company with the TVR, the Glamorgan Canal, two roads and the Pentyrch Railway, and over the top of them all strode the Walnut Tree Viaduct of the Barry Railway. Not content with that, the region was presided over by Castell Coch, a medieval fortress recreated for the Marquis of Bute. I cannot linger here any more. A massive trunk road interchange carved the valley up in 1971 destroying much of the magic of the place. Castell Coch Tunnel, through which I rode on 155, was bulldozed out of existence.

LEFT: The quiet decay of the Rhydyfelin line at Castell Coch Tunnel, Tongwynlais, after final abandonment in 1952. Nothing speaks more eloquently of the dashed hopes and frustrated ambition of this would-be main line railway of 1911. The date over the 108 yard tunnel is 1906. The GWR reduced the CR line to single track beyond Coryton in 1928 when all hope of revival had gone. *Photo: R. J. Doran*

Cardiff-Rhydyfelin

BELOW: Back to nature at Tongwynlais station on 16 September 1949 with Traveller's Joy, Toadflax, Blackberry and Birch trees already burying the derelict loop and not a weed killing train in sight! GWR rebuilt ex Rhymney Railway 0-6-2T 66 is heading a train of equipment for Nantgarw Colliery which was reopened by the National Coal Board in 1950. *Photo: Ian L. Wright*

ABOVE: Another ex RR engine, GWR 41, brings
coal up the Cardiff Railway to the new Nantgarw
Coke Plant on 3 January 1952. The train is crossing
the Glamorgan Canal for the third time, at Glan y
llyn. On 16 June 1952 a new double track connection
was opened to the nearby TVR main line at Taff's
Well enabling the Tongwynlais portion of the CR to
be abandoned. *Photo: Ian L. Wright*

Ynysybwl Branch

Pontypridd was the focus of five branch line passenger services, in addition to the Merthyr and Rhondda trains, and this goes some way to explain why Pontypridd's long curving island platform, remodelled in 1907, was so indented with bays. In 1930 the branches worked from Pontypridd by the GWR were those to Llantrisant, Old Ynysybwl, Nelson, Machen, and to Cardiff (via St. Fagans), and, except for the service to Nelson which disappeared in 1932, all these trains were still delighting the branch line enthusiast until 1952. They were byways of great character.

BELOW: On 26 July 1952, the last day of the Ynysybwl passenger service, GWR auto fitted 0-6-0PT 5421 stands in the Taff Vale 'motor car bay' at Pontypridd attached to GWR ex steam railmotor trailer 103 for the 5.34 pm departure to Old Ynysybwl Halt. GWR ex TV Class A 0-6-2T 371 is

ORIGIN:	**Taff Vale Railway**
LENGTH:	**4m 69ch Clydach Court Junction-Llanwonno**
OPENED:	**1885 (Freight)**
	1 January 1890(Passenger: Abercynon-Ynysybwl)
	30 May 1900 (Freight: Clydach Court Loop)
	17 October 1904 (Passenger: Clydach Court Loop)
	(Passenger: Ynysybwl-Old Ynysybwl)
CLOSED:	**28 July 1952 (Passenger)**
	Freight closed in stages 1931-1959 between Llanwonno and Lady Windsor Colliery. Last coal train ran Lady Windsor Colliery-Stormstown Junction on 20 May 1988. Branch is out of use (June 1988).
RULING GRADIENT:	**1 in 40**

on a Merthyr passenger turn while 6661 waits in the adjoining bay. *Photo: R. C. Riley*

LEFT: A DMU railtour visits Ynysybwl in the rain on 11 July 1959. Some container traffic is in the yard. Closure to freight, Ynysybwl to Windsor siding, came on 2 November 1959 and none too soon by the look of the track. The road on the right is the run round loop. *Photo: Ian L. Wright*

In 1885-86 the Lady Windsor Colliery was sunk by David Davies & Co in the rural valley of the river Clydach at Ynysybwl and a busy community grew up there. The TVR built a mineral branch up the valley to Llanwonno from a junction with their main line at Stormstown, this junction trailing in towards Abercynon. A TVR source gives the opening date at 1885 but a GWR date is a year later. A service of ordinary trains was put on between Ynysybwl and Abercynon on 1 January 1890, but with the opening of the Clydach Court Loop in 1900 a shorter journey was possible direct to Pontypridd.

The one and only station on the branch was at Ynysybwl. It was built on a cramped site with a single platform and goods yard on the up side and a curving gradient of 1 in 51 rising to Llanwonno. To find room for the railway the contractors had to divert the river through a tunnel excavated in the Pennant rock. On 17 October 1904 the TVR started a motor car service of steam railcars between Pontypridd and Old Ynysybwl. The platforms, only 40 feet long and with no shelters, were put in at Berw Road (main line), Robertstown and Old Ynysybwl. Later two more were added, at New Road (1910) and at Clydach Court (1915)

Few Welsh branch lines could have produced a more off-the-beaten-track location than Old Ynysybwl halt, the terminus of the TVR and GWR auto service. This community, half industrial, half rural, is the gateway to a more remote part of the valley and for generations local people have called it "the old Bwl". Guard Green, a regular guard with a devilish sense of humour, enlivened many journeys up the branch. According to him, one day on Pontypridd station, he outraged several women shoppers with the call "Anymore of you ladies for the Old Bwl?"

The line continued under the bridge to Mynachdy Colliery and on to Cwm siding where there was a stone faced wharf for agricultural traffic. It continued to the 800 foot contour, crossing and re-crossing the Clydach, but the small drift mines it served had all stopped working early this century. The GWR lifted the track beyond Mynachdy in 1938. A TVR working timetable of May 1913 emphasised caution on the gradients: "Above Ynysybwl the engine must invariably be at the Ynysybwl or lower end of the train."

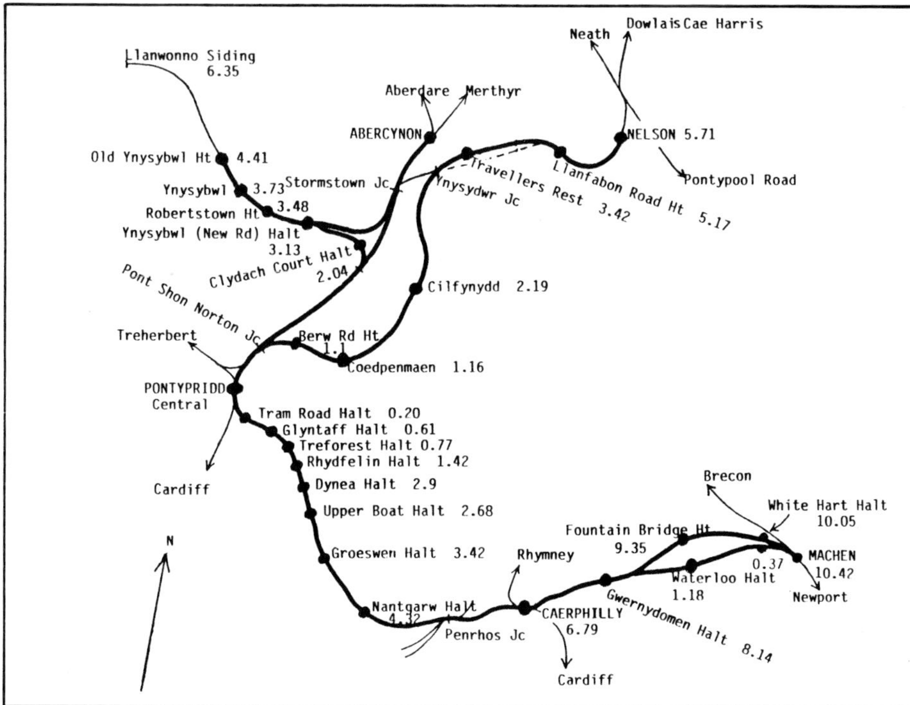

Ynysybwl Branch

RIGHT: Guard Green and passengers converse during rural moments at Old Ynysybwl Halt on 25 May 1946 as GWR 0-6-0PT 6416 of Abercynon shed simmers with the branch auto train. Arrangements at Robertstown Halt were less civilised. Intending passengers were penned in a gated enclosure until unlocked by the guard, an anti social requirement of the Board of Trade. *Photo: Ian L. Wright*

YNYSYBWL BRANCH.

Up Trains. Single Line—   **Week Days Only.**

Clydach Court Junction and Windsor Siding. / Stormstown Junction and Windsor Siding. / Windsor Siding and Ynysybwl. } Electric Train Staff.

Ynysybwl and Old Ynysybwl. / Old Ynysybwl and end of Branch. } Train Staff. One engine in steam.

Mineral Line only.

Mile Post Mileage from Cardiff Docks M.	C.	Distance from Pontypridd Pass. Station M.	C.	STATIONS.	Station No.	Gradient 1 in	Point to Point Times.	Allow for Stop.	Allow for Start.
16	28	3	34	**Abercynon**	7552	692 F			
—	—	—	—	Stormstown	7972	348 F			
12	74	—	—	**Pontypridd** (Central)	7610	277 R			
14	61	1	67	Clydach Court Junction	7966	412 R	—	—	1
14	78	2	4	Clydach Court Halt	7649	47 R	—	—	—
15	73	2	79	Darranddu	—	66 R	—	—	—
16	3	3	9	Windsor Siding	7965	56·R	10	1	1
16	7	3	13	Ynysybwl (New Road) Halt	7676	66 R	—	—	—
16	42	3	48	Robertstown Halt	7667	66 R	—	—	—
16	67	3	73	**Ynysybwl**	7638	51 R	4	1	1
16	77	4	3	Ynysybwl Quarry Siding	7970	51 R	—	—	—
17	35	4	41	**Old Ynysybwl Halt**	7663	69 R	2	1	1
17	66	4	72	Mynachdy	—	40 R	1	1	

STATIONS.	B Auto Passenger arr. A.M.	B Auto Passenger dep. A.M.	K Goods. J6 arr. A.M.	K Goods. J6 dep. A.M.	B Auto Passenger arr. A.M.	B Auto Passenger dep. A.M.	B Auto Passenger arr. A.M.	B Auto Passenger dep. A.M.	B Auto Passenger arr. A.M.	B Auto Passenger dep. A.M.	B Auto Passenger arr. P.M.	B Auto Passenger dep. P.M.
Abercynon	..	..	—	6†50	..	..	..	..	..	..	..	..
Stormstown	....	....	6†53	8 0	....	....	....	....	....	....	....	....
Pontypridd (Central)	—	7 15	..	..	—	8 40	—	10 15	—	11 32	—	12 35
Clydach Court Junction	C	S	—	—	C	S	C	S	C	S	C	S
Clydach Court Halt	—	—	~~	—	8 45	8 46	—	—	—	—	12 40	12 41
Darranddu	—	—	8 12	—	—	—	—	—	—	—	—	—
Windsor Siding	C	S	—	8 40	C	S	C	S	C	S	C	S
Ynysybwl (New Road) Halt	7 22	7 23	—	—	8 50	8 51	10 22	10 23	11 39	11 40	12 45	12 46
Robertstown Halt	7 26	7 27	..	..	8 54	8 55	10 26	10 27	11 43	11 44	12 49	12 50
Ynysybwl	7 30	7 31	8 46	9 20	8 58	8 59	10 30	10 31	11 47	11 48	12 53	12 54
Ynysybwl Quarry Siding	—	—	9 22	9 30	—	—	—	—	—	—	—	—
Old Ynysybwl Halt	7 33	—	9 32	—	9 1	—	10 33	—	11 50	—	12 56	—
Mynachdy												

GWR Service Timetable No.9 September 1928

RIGHT: The approach to Old Ynysybwl Halt was on a rising gradient of 1 in 51 easing to 1 in 59 and drivers could not afford to shut off steam until they had actually reached the halt. GWR 0-4-2T 1461, photographed on 13 March 1948, is arriving at Old Ynysybwl with the 4.22 pm auto from Pontypridd. This train was one of two that travelled the longer way via Abercynon, at morning and evening school times. *Photo: Ian L. Wright*

LEFT: Windsor Passing Siding on 25 August 1959 looking up the 1 in 56 gradient towards Ynysybwl. GWR 0-6-2T 6619, carrying the Barry 'target' B 5, is ready to move off down the bank to Stormstown with a rake of coal wagons from Lady Windsor Colliery which remained in production until closed by British Coal in March 1988. A Class 37 diesel worked the last coal train out of Lady Windsor Colliery on 20 May 1988, just over 100 years after the signing of the original TVR private siding agreement with the Ocean Steam Coal Co. The branch is today out of use and you would have to be a very observant traveller on the Merthyr 'Sprinter' to be able to spot the line trailing in at Stormstown, so thick is the encroaching screen of trees. The signalman and train crew, wandering nonchalantly on the ballast, add an element of informality to this scene from the past, with its tablet catching apparatus and romantic Taff Vale signalbox. *Photo: Michael Hale*

Nelson Branch

BELOW: Nelson Station TVR about 1910. The branch continued under the bridge to the goods yard and the GWR at Llancaiach Junction. No trace of the station remains, and ironically, the site has become a bus station. *Photo: T. J. McCarthy Collection*

The Taff Vale Railway, opened between Cardiff and Merthyr in 1841, was early on the scene with a mineral branch from Stormstown near Abercynon eastwards to collieries at Llancaiach. A TVR minute recorded that the line was "to be worked by horse power and to be opened on 25 November 1841, no passengers to be carried." One would hope not, in view of a hair raising 1 in 11 cable operated incline near Traveller's Rest. The contractors who started the construction were Storm & Douglas. It was Storm who seems to have given his name to Stormstown Junction and Douglas to "Pont Douglas", a long vanished bridge over the incline. Under an Act of 1873 the Llancaiach Branch was realigned on an easier gradient but it remained out of use until 1890. The new Dowlais Colliery then being sunk at Abercynon seems to have received construction materials from the Dowlais Iron Co by this route, via the Taff Bargoed Joint Line and Llancaiach. The line followed a rugged terrain with mountain sheep for company as it climbed the edge of Craig Evan Leyshon Common. Above it, on a higher alignment, the route of the old incline provided a breezy walk towards Nelson.

Meanwhile, more colliery development was going on at Cilfynydd where the Taff Valley opens out into a wide flood plain and in 1887 the TVR opened a branch from its main line at Pont Shon Norton Junction to Albion Colliery, Cilfynydd. An iron viaduct carried this branch over the Taff at the celebrated Berw Falls, a popular venue for early 19th century travellers on picturesque tours before industrialisation of the valley.

Passenger trains came late to the Nelson Branch, in 1900. In that year the Cilfynydd line was extended up the valley to meet the 1873 Llancaiach Branch at Ynysydwr. Stations were provided at Coedpenmaen, Cilfynydd and Traveller's Rest and a service of steam railcars put on between Pontypridd and Nelson TVR with halts later being added at Berw Road and Llanfabon Road. The branch was single, being worked by electric train staff with an intermediate crossing loop at Cilfynydd. A curious feature here was that the loop was some distance south of the station. Nelson and Cilfynydd were the only stations with goods yards and one daily goods train was sufficient for local needs on the branch.

Though I have been familiar enough with the empty cuttings and embankments left behind by the Nelson Branch, I have to admit that the last train to Nelson left Pontypridd long before I began to take a serious interest in exploring railway byways. Tantalisingly few photographs of the railway seem to exist at all. One of the compelling sights of the past must have been the Llanharry to Dowlais iron ore trains which were worked over the L&TV and Nelson lines by Llantrisant men as far as Llancaiach. There were two a day over the branch in 1928, hammering fully loaded against the 1 in 40 through Traveller's Rest. Passenger trains did not serve Cilfynydd all that well. A linear settlement, Cilfynydd had developed along the main road and fighting a losing battle against Pontypridd's electric trams, the GWR auto trains gave up the struggle in 1932. The track beyond Cilfynydd was lifted in 1936, but coal traffic from Albion Colliery continued until September 1970.

LEFT: Albion Colliery, Cilfynydd, seen from the northern junction with the Nelson Branch, which was being visited by a special charter railtour on 11 July 1959. The valley is seen looking south to Pontypridd. *Photo: Ian L. Wright*

Up Trains.   NELSON (Glam.) BRANCH.   Week Days only.

Single Line Pont Shon Norton Junction and Llancaiach Junction, worked by Electric Train Staff. Staff Stations—Pont Shon Norton Junction, Cilfynydd Loop, Nelson. Crossing Station—Cilfynydd Loop.

M.P. Mileage from Cardiff Docks		Distance from Pontypridd.		STATIONS.	Station N°.	Gradient. 1 in	Point to point times.	Allow for Stop.	Allow for Start.	B Workmen's Passenger. arr.	dep.	B Passenger. arr.	dep.	J Goods. arr.	dep.	F 7.55 a.m. Llantrisant to Ffaldcaiach Iron Ore. arr.	dep.			B Passenger. arr.	dep.
M	C	M	C							A.M.	A.M.	A.M.	A.M.	A.M.	A.M.	A.M.	A.M.			A.M.	A.M.
12	74	—		**Pontypridd** (Central)	7610	277 R	—	—	—	—	5 43	—	6 57	..	..	..	..	..	..	—	11 25
13	56	0	62	Pont Shon Norton Junction	7960	L	—	—	2	C	S	C	S	—	8 16	9 46B	E 9 53	....	...	C	S
13	75	1	1	Berw Road Halt	7646	430 F	—	—	—	5 45	5 46	6 59	7 0	—	—	—	—	..	..	11 27	11 28
14	67	1	73	Cilfynydd Loop Junction	7962	L	—	—	—	C	S	C	S	C 8 22	S	C	S	....	...	C	S
14	70	1	76	Albion Colliery Lower Junction	..	287 F	4	. 1	1	—	—	..	..	—	—	—	—	..	..	—	—
15	13	2	19	**Cilfynydd**	7569	103 R	—	—	—	5 50	5 51	7 4	7 7	—	—	—	—	...	...	11 32	11 33
				Stormstown Junction	7972	178 R	—	—	—	..	..	..	..	..	..	..	..	..	..	..	..
16	19	3	25	Ynysydwr Junction	....	40 R	—	—	/	5 55	5 57	7 11	7 12	—	—	—	—	....	...	11 37	11 38
16	36	3	42	**Traveller's Rest** (Abercynon Upper)	7673	40 R	—	—	—	6 1	6 2	7 16	7 17	—	—	—	—	....	...	11 42	11 43
18	11	5	17	Llanfabon Road Platform	7658	264 R	—	—	—	—	—	—	—	—	—	..	..	..	..	—	—
18	41	5	47	Berthgron Siding	7963	550 R	—	—	—	6 4	—	7 19	—	—	—	10 12	10 17	....	...	11 45	—
18	65	5	71	**Nelson** (Glam.)	7599	857 R	—	—	—					8 39	—	—	—	..	..		
19	1	6	7	Nelson Goods	7965	215 R	15	1	—						X a	10 20	10 25				
19	12	6	18	Llancaiach Junction	....	215 R	—	—	—	....	....	....	....		Z 3	—	—	....	....	....	....

No. 9.

GWR Service Timetable No.9 September 1928

Pontypridd-Machen

If you had wanted to experience for yourself the competitive complexity of the South Wales railway scene you could not have done better than take the branch train over the PC&N line from Pontypridd to Machen. On that run of only 10½ miles the auto train passed over or within sight of the lines of six Welsh railway companies — the Taff Vale, the Cardiff, the Alexandra Docks, the Barry, the Rhymney and the Brecon & Merthyr Railways, all of which were absorbed by the GWR in 1922.

The initials PC&N stood for Pontypridd Caerphilly & Newport Railway, a line built under Acts of 1878 and 1883 and opened between Pontypridd and Penrhos Junction in 1884 and between Bassaleg and Alexandra Docks, Newport, in 1886, with the object of diverting Rhondda coal to Newport for shipment rather than Cardiff. In 1897 the PC&N was absorbed by the extravagantly titled Alexandra (Newport & South Wales) Docks & Railway, but a little piece of history — the nameplate ''PC&N Junction'' on the signalbox at Pontypridd — was still in situ in the 1950s, recalling the old company.

Pontypridd-Machen auto trains, usually in the hands of an Abercynon 6400 class pannier tank, climbed easily out of the Taff Valley on a gradient of 1 in 200. This part of the line was best appreciated, I always thought, from 900 feet up on Craig yr Allt where the gently winding double track, spread out like a map below, added its mark to the pattern of field boundaries along the edge of Mynydd Mayo. Turning eastward at Nantgarw the train made for a cleft in the hills to Penrhos where it passed into the Rhymney Valley over 1¾ miles of the former RR to Caerphilly.

ORIGIN:	**Pontypridd Caerphilly & Newport Railway**
	Alexandra (Newport & S. Wales) Docks & Railway
	Rhymney Railway Brecon & Merthyr Railway
LENGTH:	**10m 42ch**
OPENED:	**November 1859 (Freight: Penrhos Jc-Caerphilly Jc) (RR)**
	1864 (Freight: Machen Jc-Caerphilly Jc) (B&MR)
	7 July 1884 (Freight: Pontypridd PCN Jc-Penrhos Jc)
	28 December 1887 (Passenger: Pontypridd PCN Jc-Newport)
	1 November 1890 (Freight: Gwaunybara Jc-Machen Jc)
	(Machen Loop via Fountain Bridge)
	14 September 1891 (Passenger: Gwaunybara Jc-Machen Jc)
	(Machen Loop via Fountain Bridge)
CLOSED:	**17 September 1956 (Passenger: Pontypridd PCN Jc-Machen Jc)**
	20 July 1964 (Freight: Machen Jc-Gwaunybara Jc)
	(via Waterloo)
	2 January 1967 (Freight: Glyntaff-Penrhos Jc)
	31 July 1967 (Freight: Glyntaff-Pontypridd PCN Jc)
	20 November 1967 (Freight: Caerphilly East Jc-Machen Jc)
RULING GRADIENT:	**1 in 39**

LEFT: Two types of passenger service were worked over the Pontypridd-Machen line; a through Newport High Street-Pontypridd service started by the ADR in 1887 and a purely local service of railmotors put on in 1904 between Pontypridd (Tram Road) and Caerphilly and later extended to Machen. Calling at one of the seven ground level halts with a Caerphilly train in 1921 is the Alexandra Company's Wolverhampton built 0-4-2T 14, bought as GWR 1426 in 1911 to replace the ADR's two steam railmotors. The GWR were to get 1426 back again at the grouping and she regained her old number! The rolling stock seen here is of the greatest interest. Clerestory roofed steam railmotor conversion No.2 is followed into Rhydyfelin Halt by a coach from the Barnum & Bailey circus tour train. *Photo: Brian Miller Collection*

BELOW: Apart from the closure of the halts at Tram Road and Glyntaff, not very much changed during the GWR regime. McKenzie & Holland semaphores were replaced by products from Swindon, but a tiny hipped roof ADR signalbox survived at Groeswen Halt on 7 May 1948 as 6401 runs in with an afternoon auto for Machen. The auto set is made up of Rhymney open third 1079 and driving trailer 103. *Photo: Ian L. Wright*

Pontypridd-Machen

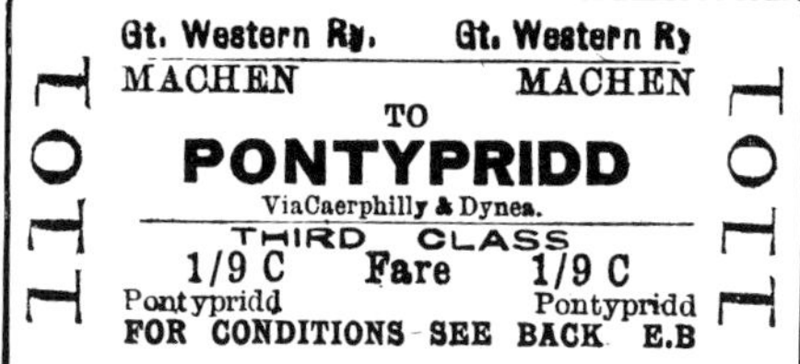

The local trains serving the halts between Pontypridd and Caerphilly ran almost without alteration for 52 years. One curiosity was the ADR halt at Tram Road, just short of PC&N Junction Pontypridd. All railmotor passengers were deposited there and had to walk the rest of the way to Pontypridd TVR. It has been said that the TVR had banned the ADR's trains from Pontypridd station. Others declare that the ADR refused to pay the junction and station charges. All this, of course, was ironed out when the GWR took over in 1922.

Glyntaff, the ADR Company's northern HQ, was laid out in a precipitous quarry. From its summit was a bird's eye view of the goods yard, engine shed, carriage sidings and Glyntaff halt, with a commanding panorama of Treforest.

TOP: Halfway point on the Pontypridd-Machen run was Penrhos Junction, among the hills to the east of Nantgarw. Set in a defile to the west of Caerphilly, the Penrhos region was the focus of three railway routes. First of these was the old Rhymney Railway main line, centre, whose 'Big Bank' ran down a 1 in 47 gradient to Walnut Tree Junction to meet the TVR. Next, right, are the PC&N lines running west to Pontypridd. Diverging, left, at the signal box is the Barry Railway, and over the top of them all, centre, are the abandoned piers of the BR's Rhymney Branch opened in 1905 and closed in 1926. Penrhos Junction was photographed in April 1957 looking west. A Taff's Well banker gives a helping hand to an empty Rhymney Valley mineral train which has just reached the top of the 'Big Bank'. *Photo: Ian L. Wright*

BOTTOM: Caerphilly station on 2 September 1959 looking towards Pontypridd. The Machen branch trains used platforms 3 and 4, right, while the Rhymney-Cardiff services continue to run from 1 and 2, left. A bus station has now been built on the branch platform site. *Photo: Michael Hale*

The Pontypridd-Machen auto left the Cardiff-Rhymney main line at Caerphilly East Junction and turned sharply away on a double track falling gradient towards Machen. Now in these fields and farmlands beside the river Rhymney at Gwaunybara the Machen line sprang one of the railway surprises of Wales. The down line diverged from the up line to form the Machen Loop, easing the gradient of 1 in 39 on the old line to 1 in 200/68 on the new, and making things easier for the coal trains to Newport. Possibly uniquely, the two single lines of the loop were served by halts ¼ mile apart. Fountain Bridge was on the 1890 loop and was in Monmouthshire, served by Machen trains only. Waterloo, on the 1865 line, was in Glamorgan and served by trains in the Caerphilly direction only. In this unidirectional situation a passenger buying a return ticket from the guard at Waterloo would expect to be brought back to Fountain Bridge! Unlike its well known London counterpart, this Waterloo had no more accommodation than two sleepers, a length of fencing, a nameboard and an oil lamp, with an additional oil lamp facing Machen to help the driver home-in on the place after dark.

BOTTOM: An afternoon Pontypridd-Machen auto train hauled by 6438 displaying the Abercynon 'target' JE, runs into the rail level halt at Fountain Bridge in 1955. *Photo: Rev R. W. A. Jones*

With the arrival of the branch train at Machen this survey ends, where it began, on the Brecon & Merthyr line. We have been here before in an earlier page in this book. Housing development and road widening have covered the track at Machen now, but indelible images of the train journey remain in the memory. The ride in the front of the auto on the way back to 'Ponty', the elderly ladies at Groeswen going into Caerphilly for the shopping; the jokes of the companionable Guard Green and the slam of the lever as the halt steps were retracted on the trailer. All these things are not easily forgotten.

The train departure board at Pontypridd showing main and branch services from the station in the GWR timetable for 1 October 1945. The blank space represents the only closure at that date — the vanished service to Nelson. From the grouping until 1930 the GWR named this station Pontypridd Central to distinguish it from the Barry Railway station at Pontypridd Graig. *Photo: Ian L. Wright*

ALSO AVAILABLE

BRANCH LINE BYWAYS Vol.1 The West Midlands
by G.F. Bannister

BRANCH LINE BYWAYS Vol.2 Central Wales
by G.F. Bannister

OUR NEW MAGAZINE

In 1986 Atlantic published the first issue of BACKTRACK, a high quality quarterly devoted entirely to British railway history and incorporating a number of unique features. Each issue includes: 12 large pages of *full colour* historical photographs; an article on *each* of the 'Big Four' railway companies (or respective BR region); a branch line article; plus a wealth of other well-researched material on British railway practice over 150 years up to the mid-1970s. BACKTRACK is on sale in major newsagents and selected specialist railway and model retailers. For a sample copy send £2.25 to the address at the front of this book.